HIGH GOTHIC

HIGH GOTHIC

The Classic Cathedrals of Chartres, Reims, Amiens

by

HANS JANTZEN

Translated from the German by
JAMES PALMES

PRINCETON UNIVERSITY PRESS
Princeton, New Jersey

Published by Princeton University Press, 41 William Street,
Princeton, New Jersey 08540

Copyright © Rowohlt Taschenbuch Verlag GmbH, Hamburg,
1957
English Translation 1962 by Constable and Co. Ltd.

High Gothic was originally published under the title *Kunst der
Gothik* as part of the series 'rowohlts deutsche enzyklopädie'
edited by Ernesto Grassi

First Princeton Paperback printing, 1984

LCC 83-43099
ISBN 0-691-04026-5
ISBN 0-691-00372-6 (pbk.)

Reprinted by arrangement with Pantheon Books, a Division of
Random House, Inc.

Princeton University Press books are printed on acid-free paper,
and meet the guidelines for permanence and durability of the
Committee on Production Guidelines for Book Longevity of the
Council on Library Resources

Printed in the United States of America

9 8 7 6 5 4

CONTENTS

Contents

INTRODUCTION

The Gothic World and the Present Day

WHAT WE term Gothic does not imply a monument or
work of art of a particular kind, either in architecture
or the other visual arts. Thirteenth-century Gothic does not
look the same as the Gothic of the fourteenth and fifteenth
centuries. Yet, whatever the manner of its interpretation,
all Gothic art seems to have a common denominator, which
has its roots in a certain fundamental attitude of Western
man, determining his behaviour towards the divine world of
Christian belief and the natural world about him. As a historical phenomenon Gothic spread from the land of its birth in
Northern France to become the sacred style of Europe, but
with differing shades of expression, which reflect the contributions of individual countries and peoples.

Although the Gothic age lies far in the past, its creations
have profoundly influenced the life of the present. Despite
wars and revolutions, reformations, divisions and deviations
in religious belief, there survive in every European country
an incalculable number of Gothic cathedrals, minsters and
churches, in which God is still worshipped. Even the vest-
ments and liturgical furniture of these churches are often
characterized by features peculiar to the Gothic grammar of
form. But if so many tangible monuments of the Gothic
centuries surround us, the key to their artistic and religious
inspiration is hard to find. Mediaeval Christendom has gone
for ever. In the course of time Gothic forms of expression
have changed their values. They were long regarded as an
aberration of Western art, a sign of barbaric taste. And what
devastation has been caused by the effects of these spiritual

crises, not least in the French revolution, when men tried to remove the evidences of the Christian middle ages! At Reims the church of St. Nicaise, one of the finest examples of French Gothic, was demolished, and at Cambrai the Gothic cathedral was destroyed. The cathedral of Strasbourg was proclaimed a temple of reason and its sculptured figures defaced.

Today we admire Gothic cathedrals, and yet, with our twentieth-century mentality, we lack any true basis for comprehending them. Even when they are preserved in a material sense, their spiritual significance seems completely hidden. Moreover, we have no real understanding of the standards which made them works of art, for we are not "cathedral-minded" any more. That is easy to see, because we can no longer build Gothic cathedrals, even when we wish to do so. Nineteenth-century church architecture tried, and failed lamentably. An insuperable barrier indeed separates their approach to building from ours, but chronicles survive to tell us of the spirit in which cathedrals were built in the twelfth century. Robert de Mont-Saint-Michel recorded[1] in 1144:

"In that year were to be seen for the first time at Chartres the faithful harnessed to carts, laden with stones, timbers, corn and whatever might be needed for the work of building the cathedral, the towers of which rose like magic into the heavens. And this was happening, not only here, but almost everywhere in France and Normandy and in other parts. Everywhere men humbled themselves, did penance, and forgave their enemies. Men and women could be seen dragging heavy loads through mire and marsh, praising in song the miracle which God was performing before their eyes."

Abbot Haimon of St. Pierre-sur-Dives in Normandy wrote to the Prior of his order at Tutbury in England:

"Whoever saw or heard the like? Lords and Princes, full of riches and honours, even women of noble birth, their proud heads bowed, harnessed like beasts of burden to carts, bringing wine, corn, oil, lime, stones, timbers and other things needful for sustaining life or the fabric of churches.

[1] Cf. Dehio-Bezold, *Kirchliche Baukunst des Abendlandes*, VI, page 22.

And though more than a thousand people are there, deep silence reigns, no word is heard, not even a whisper. Nothing can stop them. You would think that you were witnessing the Jews of old striding over Jordan. The very sea is held back to let them pass, as eye-witnesses of Sainte-Marie-du-Port have asserted. When the pilgrims reach the church which they want to help to build they form a camp of their waggons and watch, and sing psalms, the whole night through. On every cart candles and lamps are lit, relics are brought to the sick, and processions of prayer are held for their recovery."

The attitude of our time towards building is very different. Cathedrals were the tower blocks of the Gothic city. Nowadays tall buildings are no longer devoted to sacred purposes. Here is a typical report of the erection of a high building in a modern city:

"It is anticipated that work should be completed on the construction of the new *Daily Mirror* building before the end of the year, although it may be some time after that before the printing presses have been completely installed and tested. This huge block has eighteen floors in its central tower section, four of them below ground level, and is the second largest postwar building in London. The roof is 169 ft. above ground and the basement is 46 ft. below ground, involving excavation to a depth of 60 ft. and the moving of 126,000 tons of soil. Much of the 2,500,000 cu. ft. basement space is taken up by the huge printing presses on which it is planned to print the whole of the 14,000,000 circulation. The ten acres of floor area, giving a total volume of 6,700,000 cu. ft., will house a working population of approximately 3,000 people. As there is no garage in the new building another building is being erected on an adjacent site to the south with a garage capacity sufficient for both blocks. It is anticipated that the office space in the second building will be let out.

"The size of the building meant that in places the retaining walls had to be 5 ft. 6 in. thick and the column diameter at basement level is 4 ft. 6 in. with the columns spaced at 45 ft. intervals in each direction. The maximum load per column is 2,800 tons and the maximum floor area per column is approximately half an acre. It is estimated that during construction some 93,000 tons of concrete and 6,000 tons of reinforcing steel will be used."

(From *The Civil Engineer*, July 1959.)

The difference between these accounts is a measure of the gap between ourselves and the cathedrals of the thirteenth century. But it is not so wide that we do not visit and admire them, for they are a part of our Western world, evidence of a religious society whose places of worship must be reckoned among the most important architectural achievements of Europe. To appreciate them it is essential to become acquainted with their structural features in detail, to grasp their tremendous size and strict organization, in fact to examine them closely without, in so doing, losing sight of the majestic richness of their whole conception.

The Concept of the Gothic Cathedral

A study of Gothic cathedrals is not at all the same thing as a study of Gothic church architecture. Not every Gothic church is a cathedral, which indeed represents only a certain type of Gothic church. Name and rank were determined in the first instance by the hierarchy of the priesthood. The cathedral was the church of a bishopric. It was thus distinguished in the Gothic system from other types of parish and abbey church by a particular measure of artistic grandeur, as an expression of a certain ecclesiastical eminence and power. In different countries the description "cathedral" for a bishop's church is not employed uniformly, nor does terminology vary logically according to the Germanic and Romance lands. Throughout France, Spain and England a bishop's church is a cathedral. In Germany there is no such designation. "Dom" or "Münster" are the terms. Similarly, in Italy "il duomo" is used.

The description "Gothic cathedral" implies in addition an allusion to the historical importance of this type, to the extent that the cathedrals, as bishops' churches, represented the advanced theories of Western architecture. There were

"Romanesque" cathedrals, too, for example those of Périgueux, Angoulême and Cahors. But among Romanesque churches it was the great abbeys which were the leaders of sacred architecture.

Which then were the cathedrals in which Gothic principles grew to full maturity?

Where Gothic Originated

The researches of nineteenth-century art historians have identified beyond any shadow of doubt the district from which Gothic sprang. It was in Northern France and close to Paris, in Ile-de-France, Champagne and Picardy, that the first decisive steps were taken. The cathedrals of this region, like Noyon, Senlis, Paris, Laon, but also other and smaller buildings, speak an architectural language which conveys a sense of novelty in comparison with churches in the Romanesque style. This does not necessarily mean that Gothic evolved out of Romanesque architecture. Indeed, in the very regions of European ecclesiastical architecture in which the Romanesque produced its most characteristic works, central and south-west France, on the Rhine, in Lower Saxony and Northern Italy, there was no Gothic. Facts such as these cannot be reconciled with considerations of historical development. The great stylistic movements of Western art are more often intellectual creations, which in their emergence and growth at a particular time reveal innate principles of form. Gothic exemplifies just such a principle. Through the various stages of its development in the twelfth century (Early Gothic) it rose suddenly to the imposing achievements of High Gothic in the thirteenth. Only from this leap to the heights can we appreciate the magnitude and significance of the basic conception and its relationship to tradition. And so, in order to gain our first acquaintanceship with Gothic art, we must turn to the "classic" cathedrals, which, from a large number of prominent churches, emerge as the supreme products of the Franco-Gothic conception of ecclesiastical building.

The Classic Cathedrals

The cathedrals of Chartres, Reims and Amiens form a closely knit group, exemplifying those supreme artistic qualities which, diffused and modified, were to determine the characteristic style of Western art in the years that followed. In many respects they laid down a canon for the formal vocabulary of Gothic cathedrals and provided a model for the internal and external structure of thirteenth-century church building. Chronologically, too, these three cathedrals are closely connected. Chartres was begun in 1194, Reims in 1211 and Amiens in 1220.

In plan, character and execution, each of these cathedrals displays in every architectural feature common to them all its own particular individuality. In their architectural and artistic reputation we may speak of a certain rivalry between them. For Viollet-le-Duc, the most important authority on mediaeval architecture in nineteenth-century France, the purest Gothic was represented by the cathedral of Amiens, which he called "l'église ogivale par excellence". In the nineteenth century it was spoken of as the French Parthenon. This seems understandable, since we can detect in the construction of Amiens Cathedral qualities which we admire as characteristically Gothic in Gothic architecture: transparent structural clarity, soaring verticality in the interior, majestic dimensions.

Reims Cathedral often bears the title of the Queen of French churches. In fact it incorporates so much architectural perfection in the balance of the parts to the whole, in the meticulous planning of the elevations, in the splendour of the exterior, in the elegance of the buttresses, in the majestic conception of the façades and, finally, in the sculptural adornment of the portals, that we must concede its right to the rank of "Queen". Moreover, Reims is closely linked with French royal history as the cathedral where Kings were crowned.

Chartres Cathedral is set like a crown upon the mediaeval city, the outward symbol of an age-old cult of the Virgin at this spot, its graceful mass visible for many miles across the countryside. What gives this cathedral its particular prestige does not only lie in the fact that it stands first in time among these three superb sacred buildings, but because certain basic architectural principles, which determined the general character of High Gothic cathedrals, found expression in it for the first time. Reims and Amiens were in one respect followers, although certainly not in the sense that one could describe them as belonging to the school of Chartres. Jean d'Orbais (Reims) and Robert de Luzarches (Amiens) relied upon their own interpretation of a special vocabulary of form in their buildings. But in certain points of decisive significance they are derived from Chartres, and it is precisely those points which gave a new monumental character to the form of the interior. The great achievement of the master of Chartres was to have guided the Gothic cathedral to full development through the pioneer stages of the second half of the twelfth century and in so doing, ensured the status of Gothic in Europe. Georg Dehio called the Master—we do not know his name—"the most richly endowed and original mind of the entire epoch", and we must examine all his ideas if we are to grasp what his achievement means.

Finally, by a happy accident of history, Chartres is especially distinguished, because, in all essentials, this majestic building has been preserved through the hazards of the years in the form in which it was completed in the thirteenth century. Even that most illusive of constituent elements—in its effect on the interior—the sacred light of the thirteenth century, survives. Out of a total of 186 stained-glass windows, with countless figures and stories in pictures dating from the earliest period of the cathedral, 152 still transmit that sense of enchantment which a High Gothic cathedral provided.

TRANSLATOR'S NOTE

The cathedrals of Chartres, Reims and Amiens have three-stage elevations, but four stages—even five (cf. Bourges) —were common, indeed normal, in French churches of the early Gothic period. In England, however, the four-stage system of construction was rare, and there appears to be no simple English term to describe the additional intermediate gallery. I have therefore used the word "tribune", whenever reference is made to this feature. It is a French word, of course, but I suggest that there are adequate precedents for borrowing from France. Clerestory, for example, is no more than a literal, anglicized version of "clair-étage", adorned with mediaeval spelling.

PART ONE

I. Ecclesia Materialis

The Cathedrals as Built

THE FIRST question is: What is to be our line of approach to cathedral building? Positivism in mediaeval architectural research in the nineteenth century took technical construction as its point of departure and directed all its attention to the origin and development of the ribbed vault, with many valuable results. But to start from the structural technique of the cathedral is the same thing as trying to limit the art of the brothers Van Eyck—and this was formerly the practice—to the invention of oil painting. In the Gothic interior the significance of the technical means is not immediately apparent. We shall choose in consequence another line of approach beginning with the question: What were the structural resources upon which the Gothic interior depended for its effect? And from there we shall proceed to an analysis of the Gothic "wall" as a device for containing space and producing this effect. The overwhelming difficulty of our task consists in this. When we look at a cathedral, all the effects are produced at the same time, the details being understood in the immediate experience of the whole, whilst in a descriptive analysis the importance of the building's elements must be taken into account and discussed one by one.

1. THE NAVE

The Framework

THE ELEVATION of a Gothic cathedral merges into the general framework of a multi-aisled hall of basilica type section, which means that the middle aisle (nave), as the principal space, rises above the side aisles so as to receive its light from the windows above them (Figs. 1 and 2). The actual use, or should we say the choice, of this structural form was not a matter of course, nor was it decreed from the first by tradition. In the history of the Christian place of worship the basilical section has admittedly played a decisive rôle since early Christian times, but by no means held exclusive sway. The huge pilgrimage churches in France of the early twelfth century, represented by St. Sernin at Toulouse, or, in Spain, by Santiago de Compostela, renounced (as vaulted buildings) the basilical section and, in so doing, a way of introducing light which draws the gaze upwards. The same thing occurs in different forms of the hall church. But, within the structural framework of the basilica type, Christian church building led in the course of centuries to very different interpretations of style, which we shall not discuss here, until the Gothic cathedral assumed the basilica type, not only because it made possible the raising of the nave and thus achieving an effect of soaring space, but also the transformation of the interior into an area of light.

The new possibilities spring in the first place from the elevational form of the nave walls. Structurally the Gothic nave wall is among the most remarkable, deeply original and delicately contrived achievements of European architecture.

In the nave wall of Early Gothic, and of High Gothic, cathedrals are ranged in tiers a number of constituent features: at ground level are the arcades providing access to the side aisles, with one or two galleries above them and,

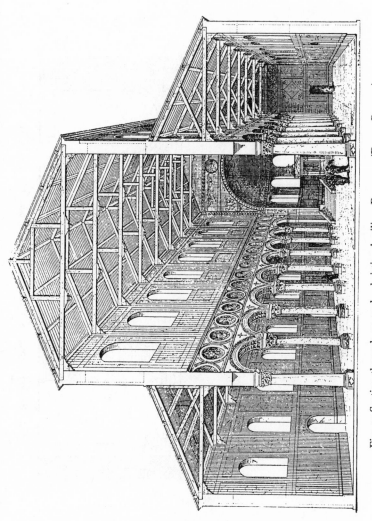

Fig. 1: Section through an early christian basilica. Ravenna (DEHIO-BEZOLD)

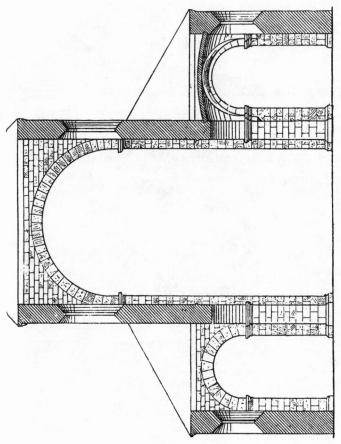

Fig. 2: Section through a 12th c. vaulted basilica. (St. Jacob, Würzburg)

finally, the windows of the clerestory. The superimposed, bay-form articulation of these features is called the elevational system (Fig. 3). It may be of three or four parts, depending on the number of galleries inserted between the arcades and windows.

The architect who designed Chartres shows a particular mastery in his handling of the "system", in which he produces a new and imposing form in the construction of the bay unit (Plate 1). Why exactly his solution is considered "a classic", and has proved itself as such, can only be understood if we first look at each separate feature of this tripartite system (arcade, triforium, fenestration) in its architectural context and also compare the infinite variety of ideas which resource ful architects tried out on French building sites in the second half of the twelfth century.

The Arcade

As soon as we enter Chartres Cathedral, the height and wide spacing of the arches, and the form of the piers separa- ting the nave from the aisles, create an impression of majestic power. The design of these arcades is the result of intuitive, but exquisite, calculation, in which nothing superfluous is allowed to appear, and in which the work and experience of two generations of twelfth-century Gothic architects is suddenly left far behind. If we are to be able to follow the ways of the master of Chartres, we must acquire some measure of understanding of the architectural problems which lay before him.

The form of arcades and of their supports underwent many changes in the history of mediaeval architecture and in the end were incorporated in the structural design of the whole nave wall. This "wall" was transformed in the course of time from the homogeneous mass of masonry of the early middle ages—the Carolingian period—from which the openings seem to have been carved out, into a composite articulated structure, from which the characteristic of mass had been eliminated. This is exactly what happened with

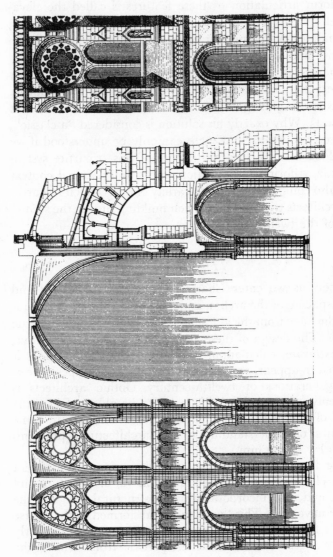

Fig. 3: CHARTRES Cathedral. Elevation and section (DEHIO-BEZOLD)

Gothic. Romanesque formed the arcade support as a cruci-form pillar which, even when provided with secondary shafts, preserves its structural unity with the solid masonry wall. Gothic does not use such pillars, since it manipulates the "wall" plastically, which in principle is sustained only by elements shaped like round bars. Early Gothic wrestled continuously with the architectural problems of the arcade supports. To understand this, it is essential to make clear how many and various are the tasks which the pier in Gothic wall construction has to perform. It has not only to afford a support for the arches, but to adopt a form which permits a series of architecturally pleasing supports throughout the length of the interior. In addition it has duties to fulfil towards the aisles as well as the nave, duties which are associated with the organization of the Gothic cross-ribbed vault. In the aisles it must carry the abutments for the side arches and diagonal ribs. On the nave side it has to cope with the vaulting shafts which rise from arcade level to prepare for the roof of the nave. What a host of functions for one architectural element!

The great Early Gothic cathedrals of Paris (Fig. 4 and Plate 53) and Laon (Plate 52) chose a cylindrical shape for the arcade piers, which rise from massive pedestals to foliated capitals, their diameter calculated to provide attractive pro-portions for the bays and an elegant series of feature for the nave.

Despite its cylindrical form we should not call this type of support a "column", but a round pier. The "column" of classical antiquity reflects totally different conceptions, with which the Gothic round support has nothing in common. The classical column obeys the laws of gravity, raising and supporting a beam placed upon it horizontally. The Gothic round pillar is a rigid structure, from the head of which spring various types of arch and shaft.

The Early Gothic round pier in Paris and at Laon has, it is true, a plain, clear cut, independent air, and solves its partic-ular problem by making all the springers of the arches and vaulting shafts of the nave rise from the grouping above the capital. But, in so doing, it strays from the fundamental

Fig. 4: Notre-Dame, Paris. Elevation I (Viollet-Le-Duc)

principle of the Gothic wall. For the over-riding logic of
Gothic architecture required that, right from the ground
plan, the containing wall of the interior should prepare for
the cross-ribbed vault. This meant the extension of the
vaulting shafts to the base of the arcade piers, which at the
same time enhanced still further the vertical emphasis of the
wall structure.

How can one "prepare" for the ribbed vault? In the nave
wall there are features, rising from the bottom to the top of
the building; in Romanesque these are projections for the
"side arches"; in Gothic, shaft-like elements, which correspond to the ribs of the vault. The question as to whether they
should start from ground level or from a higher point is
answered in different ways in Gothic. If from low down,
then they have to be attached to the arcade piers.

Round Piers and (Vaulting) Shafts

The association of a cylindrical main pillar with secondary
shafts, also cylindrical in form, exercised the ingenuity of
Gothic master masons of the late twelfth century. A column
in the classical sense of a free-standing structure cannot be
connected to other, more slender, columns. The result would
be monstrous and ridiculous. The Gothic round pier obeys
different laws, for it stands in a totally different relationship
to the building. This allows it to be joined on to adjacent
features, which do not have the same duties to perform as the
main pier. But in what context and circumstances? With
what structural considerations and visual requirements in
mind? Gothic builders pursued such problems incessantly
in order to find answers befitting their architectural theories
and the best solutions for these particular formal relationships. In the design of the arcade piers these questions played
a decisive part. Moreover, it is again characteristic of the
form of the Gothic nave wall that one cannot understand
and appreciate the grammar of the details without considering the whole composition.

Apart from the special case of the nave arcades, there are

plenty of examples in Early Gothic to show that solutions of undeniable artistry were possible for round piers faced with secondary shafts, as in the lateral aisles of the five-aisled cathedral of Paris. Here the double aisles are separated by a row of round piers, alternately plain and ringed with secondary shafts (Fig. 5).

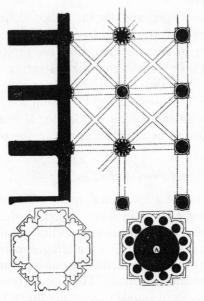

Fig. 5: PARIS, Notre-Dame. Aisle

This immediately gives a splendid rhythm to the whole sequence. It is also apparent that the relationship of the slender shafts to the cross-ribbed vault is characterized by the keenest artistic perception. The slim columns are so arranged that they by no means abandon their structural connection with the host of springers of the side arches, cross arches and diagonal ribs, but form at the same time an unbroken sequence at regular intervals about the main pier. The plan looks like the section of a ball bearing.

Alternating Piers

The alternation of piers which, in the lateral aisles of Notre-Dame in Paris, makes such a powerful appeal to the eye and the senses, conveys the structural implication of alternate supports of greater and lesser strength. In this instance, of course, one can see no structural occasion for such an arrangement. One would also expect piers of uniform proportions, corresponding to the symmetrical organization of the succession of cross-ribbed vaults. In fact the piers ringed with columns carry a heavier and, in practice, invisible load, namely the intermediate supports (originally provided) inserted in the buttress system outside. The alternation of piers in the aisles of this cathedral, therefore, reflects both structural needs and architectural principles in a vigorous, rhythmical form.

One would more easily expect from the sexpartite vaulting an alternation of piers in the arcade area of the nave, because of the different pattern of the forces of compression.

An alternation of piers of this kind in the arcade area was also by no means unfamiliar in pre-Gothic architecture and seems to have been an important aesthetic principle in the flat-roofed basilica (e.g. in Lower Saxony in the eleventh and twelfth centuries). It also appears in Early Gothic cathedrals with sexpartite ribbed vaults, used structurally now, with due regard to the compression of the vault, in the form of alternate, more and less, heavily loaded piers, as at Noyon (Fig. 6) and Senlis, where marked differences between the principal and secondary piers are the rule. The master of the Paris nave, although he was acquainted with the combination of round piers and secondary shafts, and although he used a sexpartite vault, in which after each second bay a break is made by the cross arch, has avoided the alternation of piers in the nave and forms the arcade supports uniformly of plain round piers. This also happened at Laon, but not to start with. Nothing indicates more clearly the abundance of structural ideas in the masons' lodges of those days than the experiment, in both the older bays of the nave at Laon, west of the crossing, of applying

round, shaft-ringed piers to the ground-level arches, thus
carrying the rhythmical organization of the nave wall,
dictated by the sexpartite vault, into the design of the
arcades as well, by providing an alternation of one plain, and
one shaft-ringed, pier.

It is at once clear, however, that here the architectural
problem of attaching shafts to the arcade pillars of the nave
is not quite the same as with the sequence of piers in the
lateral aisles in Paris. This is because, in the case of the

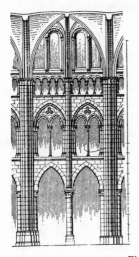

Fig. 6: NOYON Cathedral

arcade piers, the slender columns facing the nave, in their
function as vaulting shafts, extend beyond the upper part
of the round piers. The aim is to establish a link with the
nave wall by guiding the eyes upwards to the vaulting shafts,
and yet there is a hiatus in the region of the arcade supports
by the fact that the shafts are small independent columns
with their own bases and capitals, propped against the
round piers. As a result the capitals of these "colonnettes"
make a clumsy intrusion upon the design of the large, hand-
some capitals of the main piers. Moreover, how many shafts
should surround the central pier, at what intervals, and how
thick should they be? How far should the abacus project to

Fig. 7: LAON Cathedral

provide a foundation for the side arches? It is difficulties such as these which must be appreciated in order to grasp the great importance of the solutions in the classic cathedrals that follow.

In point of fact this experiment in two of the bays of Laon Cathedral was not continued in the later construction (Fig. 8 and Plate 52). From an artistic point of view the solution was obviously unsatisfactory. It was abandoned in favour of simple rows of round piers throughout the whole length of the nave. Thus the cathedrals of Laon and Paris, so different

in their basic plan and structure, are agreed in their preference for plain round supports for the arcades. They recognized that the plain round pier contrasts more effectively
with the upper parts of the wall than would a series of arches
with alternating piers, one in every two carrying secondary
shafts. In this preference is reflected an attempt, which
originates from the principles of form of the Early Gothic
nave wall in the mid-twelfth century (Noyon, Senlis), to
distribute as symmetrically as possible all the formal elements
in the entire nave wall. The problem of shaping the Franco-

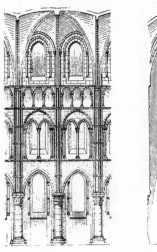

Fig. 8: Laon Cathedral

Gothic elevation lay, therefore, in bringing all formal
elements into harmony, both horizontally and vertically.
From the point of view of symmetrical rows of piers it is
natural to think of a succession of pillars encircled with
secondary shafts. English Gothic put this idea into practice.
But English Gothic did not think so "structurally" as French;
it emphasized more the decorative side, a richness and
variety in formal patterns and harmonies. In the nave of
Lincoln Cathedral and in the choir at Salisbury the polygonal piers are ringed with eight black marble columns.

The Compound Pier

These decisive and striking developments in Early Gothic nave architecture in Paris and at Laon culminated at Chartres (begun 1194) in the compound pier, the classic solution for the arcade supports (Fig. 3 and Plate 1). In contrast to Paris and Laon, by placing four large shafts about each pier in longitudinal and transverse positions on plan, the master contrived a design which fulfils and emphasizes every function of the Gothic nave pier. Rising from the foot of the arcades, the vaulting shafts of the nave now have their own support. The arcade arches stand out sharply against the wall and on the aisle side the abacus over the shaft accommodates both the springers of the cross arches and the diagonal ribs. As, however, every change in the form of details can only be understood in relation to the whole structure—here surely is the particularly French quality of "raison" and "clarté"—it must at once be noted that the master of Chartres could only bring his new conception of the arcade and of the arcade piers to fruition under two assumptions, which conflict sharply with the traditional interpretation of the Early Gothic elevational structure: (1) abandonment of the tribune gallery; (2) substitution of the sexpartite by a quadripartite vault.

We can now point to a basic difference between the Early Gothic and classic cathedrals: the longitudinal and cross-sections of Early Gothic churches like Noyon, Paris, Mantes, Senlis, Laon, the choirs of St. Rémi at Reims and of the Collegiate church of Châlons-sur-Marne show a gallery along the nave over the lateral aisles, a tribune (Figs. 6 and 8). The classic cathedrals do not have this, and the problem will engage us in the next chapter. The space previously claimed by this gallery is absorbed by the nave arcades and makes possible their impressive increase in height.

The choice of the quadripartite vault implies an even distribution of the forces of compression on the nave wall. In this the master of Chartres created the necessary condition for this type of wall system which determines its classic character: a symmetrical succession of bays throughout the entire nave and an equally symmetrical articulation of the whole wall by means of vertical shafts linking the arcade area with the vaulting.

The magnificent cathedrals of Reims and Amiens (Figs. 15 and 18) also exemplify changed values of proportion corresponding to altered conceptions of internal dimensions, and developed new ideas in details, but in their fundamental approach to elevational design they followed the principles of Chartres and, so far as the piers were concerned, gave decisive preference to the compound type (Plates 27 and 54).

With a great architect of international stature—and the designer of Chartres Cathedral must be ranked as such— every detail is important. None must be forgotten. We ought not, therefore, to leave the subject of the arcades without reference to those individual features which, in the construction of these great sequences of arches, are peculiar to him. For the symmetrical spacing of each bay unit has been so carefully considered that the piers are in fact not entirely symmetrically formed. The master may have feared that the completely unvaried repetition of one form of pier in the great arcade would be monotonous. So he made the central part of the compound pillars alternately polygonal and cylindrical, giving the auxiliary shafts the converse form, so that the cylindrical piers have polygonal shafts and vice versa (Plate 1). This gives the imposing ranks of pillars an unobtrusive, but lively, rhythm amid the austere grandeur of the cathedral architecture. Reims and Amiens did not copy this idea, but confined themselves to the cylindrical form of the compound pier (Plates 27 and 54). For the rest, the master of Chartres kept his discrete alternating pattern within strict limits. It should not be overlooked that the plinth of every pier, whether the pedestals, and piers and shafts resting upon them, are rounded or angular, is uniformly polygonal and that the formal variations occur only between the plinth and abutment. In this one particularly admires the certainty of the master in his handling of the capital with its incisive, firmly modelled foliage pattern. In the compound pier the capital grouping offers particular difficulties, because the small capitals of the associated shafts intrude upon the head of the main column. The master of Chartres solved this by treating the part of the main pier exposed between the shaft capitals as a decorated panel, even when the central pier is cylindrical in shape. Only on the nave side does he leave the secondary shaft without a true capital out of deference to its association with the vaulting shafts rising above.

In assessing the significance of the compound pier, it is natural to consider why the classic Gothic cathedrals should not have chosen the plain column exemplified in Paris and Laon. On historical evidence, however, a number of considerations discouraged such a choice. In the low "ground floors" of Early Gothic gallery churches, like Paris (Fig. 4), Laon (Plate 52), Lisieux and elsewhere, the round pillars did not have to exceed a certain height, and this was also the case in the small two-storey thirteenth-century churches of Ile-de-France. In Burgundian Gothic we find the plain round pillar used very appropriately in Notre-Dame at Dijon. But this is not a cathedral, merely a parish church of limited size. The majestic, towering dimensions of a cathedral, on the other hand, make the plain round pier seem dull, a form unsuited to the scale of the building. The cathedral of St. Étienne at Châlons-sur-Marne offers a clear example of this. The Cistercian church of Altenberg near Cologne tries indeed to rival a cathedral in size, but does not adopt the compound pier, preferring the form of the plain cylindrical support, which gives an effect of "renunciation"—a sentiment entirely appropriate to the conception of building demanded of the Order. The cathedral of Soissons occupies a midway position in this matter. Here the architect uses a fairly slender round pier, adorning it with only one shaft, which faces the nave. Although the grouping of every element in the construction of the arcade appears most carefully considered, this unconvincing solution serves only to prove that the Gothic master-mason had to develop an uncommonly acute sense of form before he was qualified to tackle the classic problems.

When we think of possible versions of the round pier,

3—HG

ornamented with shafts, from examples provided in the
history of French Gothic—and in the last resort this cannot
be done without regard for the whole elevation—we must
inevitably return in admiration to the form devised by the
master-designer at Chartres. With him everything is always
completely thought out and in full understanding of the
effect of the whole, the size of the projections, the width of
the arcades, the form of the capital grouping, where side by
side are ranged the five vaulting shafts of the nave and the
mouldings outlining the aisle arches, without gaps or overlapping. The great arches, reflecting the increased height of
the arcade, are outlined more sharply against the nave wall
(Plate i). The simple silhouette of round shaft and recessed
moulding as at Laon no longer suffices. The master of
Chartres gives the arcade the impression of being, so to
speak, independent of the wall, by placing a pointed-arched
band, drawn under the wall, upon the inner (arcade) shafts
of the compound pier. Nothing more clearly shows how
important these elevational details of Chartres were considered than the fact that the great masters of Reims and
Amiens, who followed, adopted such devices.

The Galleries

If we take the nave of Laon Cathedral as an example of the
Early Gothic elevational system (Fig. 8 and Plate 52), we
shall be impressed in particular by the skill with which the
nave wall is built up in a series of tiers. Above the great
arches at ground level is set a spacious gallery: the tribune.
The custom of using tribunes in Christian church building is
an old one, both in vaulted and flat-roofed structures, but
by no means evenly distributed, either in time or place.
They appear often in twelfth-century France. The great
barrel-vaulted pilgrimage churches on the road to Santiago
de Compostela, like St. Sernin in Toulouse or Conques,
employ them. So do the Early Gothic cathedrals in the birth-
places of Gothic in Northern France: Noyon, Senlis, Paris,
Mantes, Laon, the south transept of Soissons, the choirs of
St. Rémi at Reims and of the Collegiate church at Châlons-

sur-Marne, and elsewhere. The importance in church history
of tribunes cannot be pursued here. In the structural design
of the church they play an important rôle, both as reinforcement against the thrust of the nave vault and as
elements of the elevational system, especially when they are
combined with a small gallery, the triforium, between the
tribunes and the clerestory. This is what happens with the
four-storey system, in the analysis of which we must examine
the emergence of the triforium, which is not an undersized
tribune, but an independent feature, a kind of miniature
gallery, a corridor inserted in the wall, through which
theoretically one can pass, although otherwise serving only
as an architectural device for giving coherence to the wall
design. The triforium, as a formal element, belongs to a
category which includes all those means of bringing life to
the "dead" section of the wall between the arcade below and
the clerestory above (that part of the wall behind which
there is nothing but expanse of roof above the aisles or
tribune), and incorporating it logically in the design of the
elevation. The employment of such decorative means goes
back far beyond the elevational compositions of the Gothic
period. But even within the Gothic elevational system a wide
variety of experiments were made in the form of the wall
structure between the arcade and clerestory before the
triforium gallery proved itself in competition, as it were, as
the most effective feature for the elevation of the lofty Gothic
nave. When we think of the small two-storeyed churches of
Ile-de-France, the abundance of examples of lively architectural inspiration offered by the churches without tribunes
in the original region of Gothic compels our admiration.
On the other hand, there are three-storeyed elevations with
tribunes, but without a triforium, as in the Collegiate church
of Mantes, and galleries which look like tribunes, but open
on to dark expanses of roof, as at St. Leu-d'Esserent.

The history of elevational design in the twelfth century
follows an extraordinarily dramatic course, if one examines
in detail the changing pattern of influences which occurred
in the evolution of construction and recognizes that the road

to classic maturity is one of continuous search for the solution which is both stylistically effective and artistically flawless.

The experiments with the motif of the circle occupy a special place. In the twelfth century the cathedral of Notre-Dame in Paris displayed a four-stage elevation, which is represented by Viollet-le-Duc with one of the bays near the crossing (Fig. 4), the section of wall between tribune and clerestory being adorned with rose-windows with branching mullions. This arrangement was altered in the thirteenth century, following the precedent of the classic (High Gothic)

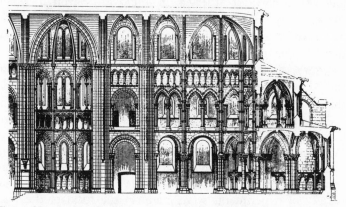

Fig. 9: NOYON. Longitudinal section through choir and crossing (transepts)

cathedrals, in favour of large composite windows. How charming can be the effect of the circular opening in enlivening the section above the tribune is apparent in the choir of a church of modest size at Chars near Paris. Here the round of the wall opening forms a boldly defined sexfoil rose.

The decisive steps, which led to the ultimate development of the triforium area, are to be found, however, in the elevations of the cathedrals of Noyon (Fig. 9) and Laon (Fig. 8).

The importance lies in the fact that at Noyon, probably modelled on the four-storey elevation of Tournai (as Georg Dehio has suggested), the triforium area is formed as a continuous series of arches, first as a blind storey, then as a passage, the wall at this stage being provided with a layer of "space". We shall refer in a later chapter to the formal significance of this continuous space layer. At Laon the important architectural factor is the particularly happy visual relationship between the triforium and the tribune galleries. Arcade, tribune, triforium and windows are super-imposed in such a way that, by subdividing the tribunes with arches, not only is an impression created of "unity in diversity" in the design of the elevational system, but, thanks to the relief effect of the architecture, of a majestic screen of sculptured latticework silhouetted against a back-ground of space. The next step forward was the three-tiered system of the classic cathedrals.

The Classic Elevational System

This stage was reached in 1194, when the master of Chartres Cathedral came upon the scene after the burning of the earlier building. The transepts and elevations under-went a startling change with his decision to do away with the tribune galleries (Fig. 3). We do not know on what grounds this action was taken. That it was decided entirely by the architect is unlikely. The clients (the bishop and chapter) must have agreed. In certain instances we have evidence that the tribunes were still used for purposes of worship. There were altars on the tribune galleries of the cathedrals of Noyon and Senlis.[1] On the other hand the use of tribunes in eleventh- and twelfth-century Western archi-tecture follows such a diverse pattern that no definite con-clusions can be drawn from their presence or absence. There are even dummy tribunes at Vignory and in North Italy (e.g., Modena), in which the openings in the upper part of the wall serve only to lighten it and to give the structure coherence. Hence we might also interpret the construction of tribunes in the twelfth century as a possible method of achieving a monumental increase in height of the nave of the larger churches without allowing the special needs of worship to interfere with the plan of the high storeys.

When one considers how conspicuously elaborate were

[1] Marcel Aubert, *Notre-Dame de Paris*. Paris, 1920. Page 90.

the gallery systems of early Gothic cathedrals, it will inevitably be realized that the abandonment of tribunes in the rebuilding of Chartres was a measure of the most daringly revolutionary kind. Probably this step reflected the directives of a higher policy, more particularly an endeavour, which was linked with the development of the Gothic cathedral as a type, to conduct the offices of worship in one place under, so to speak, a common roof, to draw the faithful away from the galleries and to gather them together in the nave, with all their attention directed towards the brilliance of the high altar and the choir.

Changes in Devotional Practice

The religious life of the middle ages was not inflexible. Even if we knew nothing of the changes which took place, we should certainly deduce from the variety in places of worship, and in the form of such places, that powerful currents flowed in the religious life of those days. The differences between Romanesque and Gothic consisted not only in the manner of building, but in the manner of participation in church services. This implied changes in devotional practice, although not in dogma. Gothic meant a new interpretation of Christian piety for the middle ages, characterized by a desire to take a more direct part in the unfolding of the sacred truths. The grandeur of the interior of the Gothic cathedral, bathed in an ethereal light, acted upon the spiritual sensibilities of believers in a different way from that of Romanesque buildings.

"The faithful were in the grip of a religious movement which impelled them actually to gaze upon the Holy Sacrament, which they were about to receive. This demand 'to see' was concentrated upon the moment when the priest takes the Host in his hands, raises it, blesses it and speaks the words of Transubstantiation; the ritual Elevation which we have found to be a more characteristic expression of Eastern liturgies, was also at that time a particular feature of the Roman Mass. Towards the end of the twelfth century we hear of visions being required at this stage in the service:

the Host shining like the sun; a tiny child appearing in the priest's hand, as he blesses the Host . . ."[1]

What this means in fact is a new attitude to devotion— actually to gaze upon the heavenly mysteries; and, when Mass is celebrated, to concentrate all the attention upon the moment when Christ is known and seen to be present. It was precisely this attitude which characterized the period when the architectural concept of the classic cathedral attained its supreme realization. The architecture of the Gothic cathedral choir went far to meet the demand for divine revelation, the ascent to the chancel, glowing with colour, representing an uplifting to the ineffable majesty of God; it constituted a vast monstrance captivating the mind and senses, and required the participant to stay within the axis of the nave in order to feel and see the mystery.

It is essential to take into consideration such changes in liturgical thinking if we are to understand the significance of the classic cathedral, which, by the abolition of the tribune galleries, led to a new spatial unity. From an architectural standpoint this resulted in an entirely new form of elevation.

In French gallery construction the tribunes imply up to a certain point a repetition of the arcades, and this is most clearly apparent when the tribune openings are not subdivided as at Noyon and Senlis. In such systems the arcade is merely one of several design features of equal value. At Chartres the arcade has no competitors. The tribunes are not there, and at once the triforium gallery assumes a new importance. It stretches like a continuous ribbon across the middle of the entire length of the nave wall, linking the bays together horizontally. This solution was to endure (Fig. 3). It became the hallmark of the classic cathedral. Reims (Fig. 15) followed the master of Chartres in this respect.

The Clerestory

However impressive the soaring grandeur of Gothic sacred architecture may seem, when we enter Chartres Cathedral,

[1] Josef Andreas Jungmann, S.J., *Missarum Solemnia*. Vienna, 1948. Volume II, page 250.

even more striking is the effect of the transformation of the interior into a supernaturally illuminated space, in which the light itself is part of the structure enclosing it. The elevations offered the master of Chartres an opportunity to achieve this result by an entirely new architectural composition for windows.

The Early Gothic basilicas of the second half of the twelfth century use simple lancet-form wall openings of modest height, corresponding to the space which the windows had to occupy in twelfth-century four-stage elevations from Noyon to Laon (Figs. 6 and 8). We must not be misled by the fact that occasionally Early Gothic cathedrals changed their window arrangement at a later phase of building under the influence of the classic solution of Chartres and Reims.

The daring with which the master of Chartres designed the clerestory was unexampled in the Europe of those days. It was sufficiently staggering that he took the gigantic measurement of about forty-five feet for the window panel, which was as high as the great arches of the nave below. But he did more. Using this dimension, he pierced the upper wall to the full breadth of the bay between the vaulting shafts with the wonderfully effective device of a composite window, comprising two lancets side by side, with a rose suspended above (Fig. 10 and Plate 1).

The circle as a window opening was, of course, known in Early Gothic, but its association with two lancets as a group and with a simultaneous increase in overall size beyond anything previously known, while also providing the framework for a great expanse of stained glass, indicated the genius of an architect ushering in a new epoch. Moreover, this rose window in the high nave of Chartres is also an elaborate architectural design, not only set out with an eight-foil pattern, but in the stone ring between the eight petals and the outer framework most skilfully contrived. In formal conception it evolved out of the great rose-window of the West Front (Plate 5), about which there will be more to say.

Architecture has always been an art in which the quality of the design is determined by proportion, all building elements, no matter what the theories which inspire them,

Fig. 10: CHARTRES. Window in the Clerestory (VIOLLET-LE-DUC)

being placed in due relation to one another. Gothic, too, laid down rules of proportion and form, which were by no means invariably mastered in every cathedral. The classic achievement of the architect of Chartres rests on his capacity to apply the correct proportion in the right place to every one of his new formal components. Not a line, profile, curve or projection can be changed without tarnishing the lustre of the whole scheme. With unfailing certainty he places the window group in the wall in such a way that the rose fits smoothly into the curved rib of the arch, with its crown touching the keystone. The individual elements, however, are not the decisive factor in the design of the elevations at Chartres, but the relationship of formal groups to one another and to the whole within a system of complete clarity and simplicity. The clerestory stands in close and unequivocal relationship to the arcade, the crowns of the arches corresponding exactly. Between the upper part of the arcade

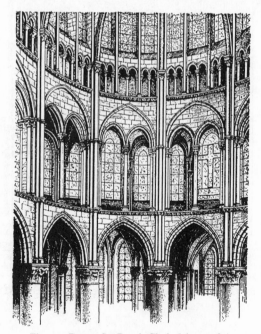

Fig. 11: REIMS, St. Remi. Choir (circa 1180)

and the windows runs the triforium like a horizontal band, in precise axial relationship to the formal design above. In the nave the triforium is divided into four-arch sequences, so that an extremely marked contrast between the triforium gallery and the dominant verticality of the bays determines the impression of the whole.

The four-tiered system of the Early Gothic cathedrals, and the choirs of Châlons-sur-Marne and St. Rémi at Reims (Fig. 11), display enchanting tracery, but courted the risk of yielding to excessive ornamentation. The architect of Chartres dismissed this danger at once by the majestic simplicity of the elevational design and austere grandeur of form. We can sense a new architectural spirit spreading across the twelfth century—the spirit of the classic cathedral.

Organization of the Vault

The method of dovetailing all the elevational elements of the Chartres Cathedral system will not be fully comprehended in its architectural implications unless we examine the function and form of the vaulting shafts. These, in their turn, will not be understood without some knowledge of the organization of the vault. The peculiarity of the Gothic nave wall, of which the most remarkable characteristic is that it consists largely of "gaps", was made possible by the use of the ribbed vault. This is not the place to discuss the structural technique of the cathedral as a whole, but the vault, which holds together the two long side walls to form the nave, must now be studied in so far as it fits into the formal arrangement of the elevational system.

The Gothic vault is a cross-ribbed system (Fig. 12). Its superiority and originality in comparison with other forms, like the barrel, ribbed and domical vaults, which were also employed in Western sacred architecture, lie in the effects of thrust and compression being absorbed in the wall structure. The diagonal, intersecting, ribs form, with the cross arches (arch ribs) and side arches, the load-bearing frame. Between the ribs and arches the web can consist of comparatively thin decking. The distribution and concentration of the stresses of the vault upon particular points and lines correspond to a systematic resolution of the wall into bearing members and infilling.

Gothic worked out and exploited these potentialities in realizing the concept of the cathedral, in which the organization of the ribbed vault depends entirely upon a predetermined ground plan, which dictates the position of the arches and ribs.

The essence of the problem is this. How can a ribbed vault be erected upon a ground plan with sides of different lengths, so that under statically correct conditions the apex of the cross arches is uniform in height with the side arches?

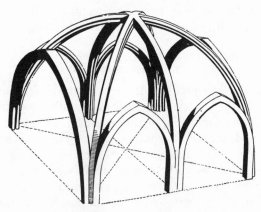

Fig. 12: Cross-ribbed vault (VIOLLET-LE-DUC)

With an equilateral plan the semi-circle provides a satisfactory solution for the side arches. As the diagonals exceed in length the sides of the square, a semi-circular arch can only be used for the diagonal ribs, if the points of support for the diagonal arches are placed lower than those for the side arches. If all these points are set at the same height, the diagonal ribs will inevitably assume a flat, and statically unfavourable, curve, if the apex of these ribs is to be equal in height to that of the side arches.

It is unnecessary to explain the history of Early Gothic vault construction in detail. Sometimes architects varied the height of the abutments in order to give the semi-circle a line

which was both visually and statically appropriate for both
the diagonal and side arches, as in the thirteenth-century
entrance of Notre-Dame at Dijon. Following this Burgundian
solution, the designer of the porch of the Cistercian church
at Maulbronn, for example, also varied the heights of the
abutments in the interests of the semi-circular lines of the
arches and ribs. Classic French Gothic found such uneven
points of support too restless. In principle, High Gothic
preferred a uniform height for all abutments. The remedy
for every difficulty of this kind in Gothic vault construction
lay in the use of the pointed arch. Only the "broken" arch
with haunches meeting in a point made it possible to achieve
an even height for the crown of the vault when the sides of
the ground plan were not equilateral. With the abutments
at the same level the diagonal ribs could now be drawn as a
semi-circle, while the side arches, thanks to the "break" of
the pointed arch form, allow the difference in height between
the crown of the vault and of the cross arches to be equalized.
The pointed arch brought liberation from dependence on a
prescribed ground plan.

The Early Gothic sexpartite vault makes the two bays
between the cross arches traversing the nave into one double
bay. The plan is divided into a series of squares (Fig. 13).
Diagonal ribs spring from the angles of the square, and an
additional rib rises to the crown of the vault from the middle
of the double bay, each square compartment being thus
composed of six panels (Plates 52 and 53). High Gothic simpli-
fied the bay sequence, forming the nave of oblong units
(Fig. 14) in place of the basic plan of the square, from which
the double bay originated. Plan and elevation are, therefore,
interdependent upon the axial relationship of the piers right
up to the crown of the vault (Plates 2 and 7). French Gothic
chose a vocabulary of form in which this interdependence of
plan and elevation finds the clearest possible expression.

The vault grips the upper wall of the nave with rod-
shaped supports which, when logically applied, extend to the
base of the arcades and mark the lines of compression. Since
they are by nature perpendicular features, they also constitute the most important elements in achieving the vertical

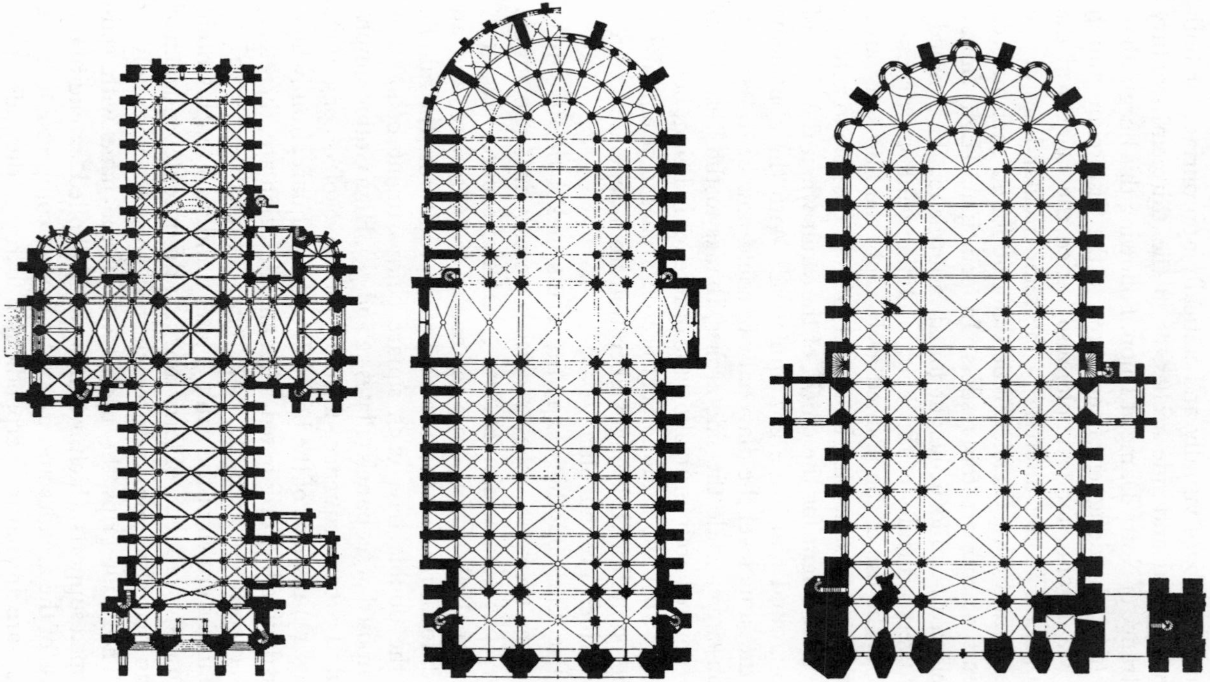

BOURGES

PARIS

LAON

Fig. 13:

effect of the nave wall, and in this respect they are by no means confined to Gothic. In pre-Gothic ecclesiastical architecture, too, perpendicular projections as supports for the cross arches in both barrel-vault structures and flat-roofed basilicas acted as connecting members. In Gothic these projections, in their association with the delicate cross-ribbed vault, are attached in the form of shafts to the nave wall. From the architectural point of view the problem to be decided lies in the degree of emphasis of such features.

The form and prominence of the shafts on the nave wall were interpreted variously according to the particular architectural character of churches. The first question was the number of shafts. When the construction was stressed in such a way that for every springing in the cross-ribbed vault a shaft was added as a support, shafts had to be provided for the cross arches, diagonal ribs and side arches. In the quadripartite vault this meant a group of five shafts, the diameter of which might be graded in size (Plates 2 and 7). With the sexpartite vault five and three shafts appear alternately, since in the double bay a cross arch is only placed above every second pier.

Construction, however, was never the deciding factor, which lay rather with the visual requirements of "style". Instead of a cluster of shafts, the Gothic architect might choose to support all the springers with a single powerful shaft, or to use three. He could equally well allow each shaft to start at a different level, at the base of the great arcade, or from the capitals, or above the triforium, or even with the arches in the clerestory.

Added to this, in the overall conception of the nave wall the meeting of the vaulting shafts with the horizontal elements of the design demands fresh consideration. How should this marriage be effected? Should these shafts rise in an unbroken vertical line over each horizontal stringcourse? Or should they combine with the horizontal features in alternating patterns of more or less sharp relief? The architect of a Gothic cathedral had countless opportunities at his disposal to make the vaulting shaft contribute to the artistic character of his design.

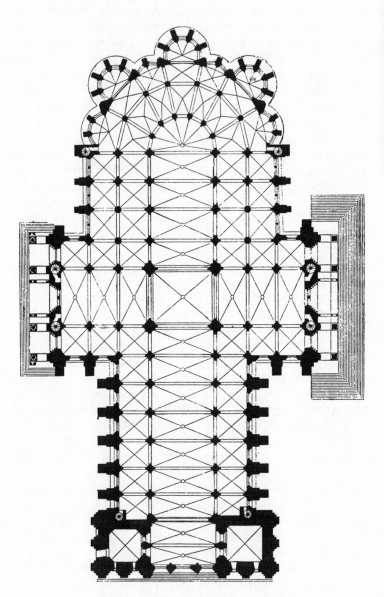

Fig. 14: CHARTRES. Plan of cathedral

Two cathedrals with high architectural pretensions, Paris and Laon, differ widely in this respect; indeed they stand in strict contrast to one another, although at ground level both use a sequence of round piers of similar shape with vaulting shafts rising only from the capitals. At Paris (Fig. 4 and Plate 53), despite the sexpartite vaults of the nave, elegantly defined shafts in groups of three soar upwards at even intervals along the nave wall, without the slightest concern for the horizontal features. The shallow curved ribs do not start until the clerestory above the capitals which surmount each group of three shafts.

At Laon (Fig. 8 and Plate 52), on the other hand, we are confronted by an extremely lively formal pattern, vigorous and rhythmical. Clusters of three and five shafts alternate, but their upward course does not run smoothly throughout. Not only do the shafts intersect the horizontal stringcourses below and above the galleries, but they are divided by rings into skilfully calculated sections, in which the height of the galleries has been taken into consideration. The shafts were also, by way of experiment, extended to the base of the great arches of the arcades in the case of alternate piers in the two older bays, but eliminated from the remainder.

The classic achievement of the master of Chartres in his design for the nave wall lies not least in the way he combined structural needs and visual effect in completely satisfying harmony. He allowed each cluster of five columns to rise from the capitals of the great arches in the absolute clarity of their function as vaulting shafts, and linked them to the base of the arcade by his creation of the compound pillar (Plates 1 and 2). It is now clear why he left the column on the nave side without a capital. In this way it appears directly related to the shaft of the cross-arch under the vault. The sensitively contrived variations in the diameter of these shafts underlines the relationship. The cross-arch shaft is more boldly defined than its neighbours for the diagonals and side arches. The dovetailing with the triforium is effected in such a way that the stringcourses at the base of the triforium gallery and below the windows are drawn over

4—HG

the vaulting shafts. The abutments for the vault are placed halfway up the great twin windows.

If we are truly to appreciate the rigorous conception of form of the master of Chartres, we must turn to English cathedrals of the thirteenth century, such as the choir of Salisbury (begun 1220), the nave of Lincoln and others. English Gothic strove for richness in details, for an impression of colourful variety, at the cost of that dominating transparent logic of French cathedral Gothic in the design of the nave wall, and fell easily into a certain excess in the decorative treatment of the vaulting shafts, a multiplicity of lines in the side arches of the arcades or of clustered columns in the galleries, tendencies which, as a basis for the cultivation of style, deviate sharply from French Gothic.

Wall and Canopy (Baldachin)

Such considerations would not be possible if we did not regard the nave wall as a continuous partition. Yet the Gothic wall has this peculiarity that, on the one hand, it is assembled by associating purely vertical units, while, on the other, it displays a tier-like horizontal arrangement of structural elements. The vertical units are characterized in their formal grouping by that phenomenon which Hans Sedlmayr has described[1] as "overlapping form" and as typical of mediaeval architectural systems. The question now arises: How are the vertical units related both spatially to their "opposite numbers" and also to their adjacent units in the wall? The connection with the opposite side is effected by the vault compartment, the link with the adjacent unit by a process of dovetailing within the structure of the wall itself. Sedlmayr stressed the link with the "opposite number" more strongly than the latter, thanks to his "canopy" theory. He based his contention upon an analysis of Justinian architecture (of the sixth century). Supports detached from the wall carry the vaulting, so that the "wall" has to be seen as a series of panels between the "canopy (baldachin)" sup-

[1] Hans Sedlmayr, *Das erste mittelalterliche Architektursystem*. Kunstwissenschaftliche Forschungen. Volume II. Berlin, 1933. Page 25 et seq.

ports, a convincing enough explanation in the examples quoted by him from ancient and Justinian architecture. "The historical importance of the creation of the canopy system", he claims, "can hardly be exaggerated. Typical buildings, not only of the Justinian period, but also of the high and later middle ages, are for the most part different forms and interpretations of this Roman-Hellenistic 'canopy' system, which in addition enjoyed a revival in an important group of post-mediaeval buildings."

However instructive the idea of the "canopy" system appears for Justinian architecture and for certain groups of later architectural systems, its transference to the Gothic interior is not a straightforward matter, since the "canopy" supports are not entirely independent of the wall. Admittedly Sedlmayr saw in High Gothic a "complete merging" of the individual canopies (baldachine), but in a "complete merging" the canopy support disappears as well. It is transformed into a hinge and the process of linking the vertical unit to its "opposite number" is reduced to a parallel movement in the plane of the wall. There are other factors which prevent us from regarding the Gothic interior as a succession of "canopy" cells. The analysis of the vaulting shaft given in the previous section is difficult to combine with the "canopy" theory. "Canopy" supports, which can be put at any height, do not fit into the conception of an independent "cell" in their relation to the wall. Moreover, especially in the High Gothic interior, it is size which speaks against the "canopy". The top of the "canopy" is so high up that it is out of physical touch and is no longer perceptibly related to individual supports. Under the crossing, it is true, one can detect signs of the "canopy"—indeed the Latin equivalent "ciborium" was used by mediaeval writers to describe this intersection of two spatial features—but this means little to the internal structure as a whole.

Let us take a familiar and famous example of Early Gothic architecture, the cathedral of Paris (Plate 53). The superbly balanced series of round piers of the arcade storey expressly rejects a system of articulation embracing from the ground up the entire wall and interior. The wall system with the sexpartite vault lies above the capitals, and indeed those characteristics which would be expected in "canopy" architecture are not apparent. The relief modelling of the wall is so sensitively handled that, supported by the bold and dignified sequence of the arcade, the unbroken evolution of the wall seems of more significance than its connection with the other side of the nave; in other words, there is no series of "canopy" cells. Sedlmayr appreciated the relationship of the arcades to the nave wall, so far as the division between them is concerned, but he explained it as a contrast of "below" and "above", with other speculations which do not carry conviction.

But even in the High Gothic system, with compound piers and quadripartite vault, the bay units are so completely merged that no canopy support in the true sense of the word could be disentangled from them. It should not be overlooked that the group of clustered round shafts not only possess the virtue of "verticality" but enter in a particular way into the relief pattern of the wall. Stylistically, the Gothic wall appears as a continuous partition composed in relief of varying depth, which asserts itself as a whole against the vertical elements and the close articulation of the bays. We shall become acquainted with further indications of this later.

Chartres and Reims

The architect of Chartres established the elevational form of the classic Gothic cathedral in its essential features. This did not mean, however, that there were to be no modifications in details. Seventeen years after Chartres Cathedral was begun the foundation stone of the cathedral of Reims was laid, the principal characteristics of the elevations (Fig. 15) emanating from the master of Chartres. The way in which arcade, quadripartite triforium and clerestory are superimposed is maintained, as are the resultant increased height of the arcade, the compound piers as arcade supports and the manner of linking the clusters of five shafts to the triforium. Where changes occur, they are connected, so to speak, with the inherent design of the classic system, but

they represent a wonderful architectural achievement and
give a new enchantment to the general character of the
cathedral. Reims means a refinement of every effect which
proceeds from architecture, in the sense of a new depth to
the system for containing space, a new harmony between
stone and stained glass, and a strong emphasis upon plastic
values in the structure of the building. Architecture and
sculpture have never stood so close to one another as at
Reims. No architectural form ever conveyed a more sculptural impression than the arcade supports of the nave; a
cylindrical central pier set about with powerful cylindrical
shafts (Plate 27). But let us begin with the changes in the
elevation. In comparison with Chartres, features which rise
do so more steeply. The arcade arches are more sharply

Fig. 15: REIMS Cathedral

pointed and their crowns touch the stringcourse beneath
the triforium. The side arches of the vault are more elegantly
defined. The arches of the triforium rise higher and are
more slender in line. The vaulting abutments are placed
lower in relation to the clerestory windows that at Chartres.

Most important of all, Jean d'Orbais, the architect of

Fig. 16: REIMS. Tracery window

Reims, designed a completely new type of window. He
achieved in fact what, since 1211 (the date when Reims
Cathedral was begun), we recognize as the "Gothic" window,
and which with the building of Reims entered upon a triumphal
progress across Europe and the centuries: the tracery
window (Fig. 16). The master of Chartres had created his
window group out of a juxtaposition of openings which seem
to be carved out of the wall. The coherent form of the wall is

maintained despite the vast extent of the breach. In Reims
Cathedral the clerestory window also occupies the entire
breadth between the vaulting shafts, but the window is
constructed within the wall opening with independent
stonework mullions and framing as "tracery", and this makes
it possible to eliminate completely the wall surface between
the vaulting supports. The individual parts of the clerestory

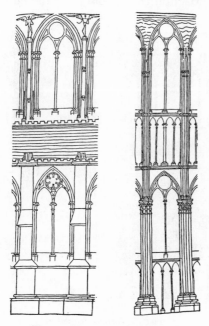

Fig. 17: VILLARD DE HONNECOURT

window of Chartres, comprising a group of two lancets and
a rose, are now merged into one lattice-like design (two
pointed arches and a six-petal rose), which is filled with
stained glass in the same manner as the wall-openings of
Chartres.

And now the architect of Reims took a step of great
consequence. He introduced his clerestory tracery windows
into the side walls of the aisles (Fig. 15). Nothing emphasizes
more sharply the difference from Chartres, where the master

had chosen for the aisles the simple lancet, preserving the solidity of the external wall in deference to the massive buttresses on the outside, about which there will be more to say later. The lighter construction of the cathedral of Reims now enabled the clerestory and arcade to be drawn into a perfectly balanced relationship by the use of similar tracery windows, without the triforium gallery losing its value as a continuous horizontal ribbon bisecting the entire elevation.

Fig. 18: AMIENS Cathedral

It is true that doubts appear to have arisen in the site workshops about the relative proportions of individual elements of the elevation to one another. In the sketchbook of Villard de Honnecourt, a peregrinating architect from Picardy who lived at the time when the great cathedrals were being built (cf. Chapter 6 on the Technique of Cathedrals), there is a drawing (Fig. 17), in which a project has been preserved for us that dates from before the building of the nave and differs in several respects from the executed plan. According to this proposal the lower part of the aisle wall

Fig. 19: Amiens Cathedral (Viollet-le-Duc)

beneath the windows was to have a row of arches, so that the socle and aisle windows would reflect the elevational scheme for the triforium and clerestory in the upper half of the nave wall. In point of fact the close association of triforium and windows in Villard de Honnecourt's drawing is not only stressed by their related proportions, but also by making the middle column of the triforium thicker than the others and thus linking it visually to the central mullion of the tracery window. With this shift of emphasis in proportions by Villard the triforium moves out of its classic middle position between arcade and clerestory—a change in values which incidentally corresponds to a later stylistic phase. Reims Cathedral, as executed, does not follow Villard's plan, but returns to the classic elevational design exemplified by Chartres.

In comparison with Chartres, the difference in the architecture of the lateral aisle wall does not consist merely in the use of the new window, but in the deep relief pattern of the wall (Plate 30). Chartres appears relatively flat. Reims not only makes the wall of double thickness to accommodate the passage, which runs above the socle in front of the windows, so that these seem to be set in niches, but is remarkable for the prominent clusters of vaulting shafts—they are in groups of seven—which stand out in a series of steps along the whole length of the socle, providing a lively sculptural effect, a vigorous piece of modelling in relief. The master of Chartres thought more simply, but not, for that reason, more meanly—austerely rather. He used clusters of five shafts over which the horizontal stringcourse at the base of the window was not extended.

Amiens

The interior of Amiens Cathedral (Figs. 18, 19 and Plate 54) reveals at once that a determination to raise the height beyond that of Chartres and Reims was the basis of the design. Since the early Gothic cathedrals the height from the floor to the keystones of the vaulting steadily increased. For Paris and Laon the figure was seventy-eight feet. It then shot

up to 118 feet at Chartres, 123 feet at Reims and 137 at
Amiens. The aisles were raised in proportion. At Reims the
crown of the aisle vaulting is fifty-three feet above ground,
while at Amiens it is over sixty. The Gothic ideal was soaring
space, the majestic dimensions inspiring awe and wonder in
the congregation.

At Amiens the arcade towers above human dimensions.
Because of its height the impression of solidity is lost and,
with it, the sense of visible "support". It is seen, so to speak,
only as towering form, a study in verticals. Even in the
triforium the vertical triumphs over the horizontal. The
upper nave walls look paper thin. As a result of these
gigantic measurements the plastic qualities of details
diminish.

The elevational system of the nave no longer follows the
original conception. Since the last decade of the thirteenth
century, the lateral aisle walls have had to give place to
chapels built between the buttresses. For the arcade Robert
de Luzarches chose once more the classic compound round
pier. Compared with Chartres and Reims, the upper nave
wall is radically altered. The tracery window of the clerestory
is doubled, thus becoming quadripartite, and the triforium is
closely linked with the clerestory and assumes a new form
as well. It now resembles windows, in that the groups of
three lancet arches are bound together by a pointed containing arch. The trefoil breach in the tympanum is combined very skilfully with the lancet arches, while the central
mullion of the quadripartite clerestory windows is extended
to the base of the triforium gallery. In comparison with
Chartres and Reims, this means that the triforium abandons
its normal position between arcade and clerestory and
becomes a formal part of the window area. A further
development in this process of associating the triforium and
clerestory was the breaching of the wall behind the triforium
and the provision of windows, thus amalgamating it completely with the clerestory as a wall of light. This happened
in the choir when it was restored after the fire of 1258.

The aisle windows remain bipartite forming a tracery
group of pointed arch and eight-petal rose.

Fig. 20: AMIENS Cathedral, exterior (DURAND)

2. THE CHOIR

THE GOTHIC cathedral interior triumphs in the architecture of the choir, the supreme culmination of its structural and artistic possibilities, the architectural expression of a transcendent event, and one which is constantly repeated, the celebration of the Mass in the sanctuary. If we seek the point of departure from which the substance of Gothic took shape, we must turn to the choir as the centre of worship. There are Gothic cathedral interiors existing only as choirs, like those of Beauvais and Le Mans, which would be sufficient alone to explain the spirit and the power and the art of Gothic. In the classic cathedrals the walls of the nave direct the gaze to the choir, the exalted, unapproachable, Holy of Holies, in which the meaning of the architecture is particularly concentrated. From the point of view of design the architecture of the choir contained a host of special requirements, and the resource and skill with which these were fulfilled must arouse the highest admiration for the architects who worked on the cathedral sites. These special requirements are also a part of a French tradition in the form of the choir of large churches. We must study the plan to understand them.

The Ambulatory and Chevet

The plan of a Gothic cathedral (Figs. 14, 23 and 24) is most commonly a sequence of nave, transepts and choir orientated from west to east, a type of layout which links the Gothic plan with countless pre-Gothic examples of Western church building from early Christian times onwards. In the middle ages, however, there developed in association with the adoration of relics in eleventh-century France a characteristic arrangement at the eastern end of a considerable number of church buildings, an arrangement at first unknown in other Western countries, in which the lateral aisles are extended round the back of the choir with chapels for the altars of the saints spreading from them outwards like a fan. This type of choir was built about 1100 at the great pilgrimage churches of St. Sernin in Toulouse, Conques and Limoges, and in the mightiest abbey church of the West, which the Benedictines built at Cluny in Burgundy. The effect produced by the choir of Cluny with its slender columns ranged in a semi-circle must have been exceptionally beautiful and imposing. Today we can only picture it in the imagination with the help of drawings, fragments, surviving capitals and reconstructions,[1] and particularly by visiting the choir of Paray-le-Monial, which reflects the architectural grace of Cluny, although on a more modest scale.

Gothic cathedral architecture adapted this motif of ambulatory and chevet chapels to its own needs and elevated it in spatial splendour to the most eloquent form of Western church design. The eastern end of the choir, terminating the long basilica, is so contrived that the open arches which bound it offer a view of the ambulatory bathed in light from the stained-glass windows of its wreath of chapels. This brilliant architectural device was first realized in the choir of the church which really initiated Gothic ecclesiastical architecture in France: the chancel of the Abbey church of St. Denis, erected by Abbot Suger and completed in 1143. Here the ground floor of the ambulatory of the choir with its chapels has survived, although the superstructure was altered in the thirteenth century. The particular beauty of the architectural solution lies in the harmonious disposition of the round piers, the handling of the Gothic ribbed vault above a trapezoidal ground plan, and the integration of ambulatory and chapels, the latter being placed so that the choir enjoys an unbroken background of coloured light. The theme was thus set which, in its architectural mastery and harmonious execution, inspired leading architects to even higher flights of originality, in accordance with varying liturgical requirements, planning conditions and site dimensions. In the rapid growth of ecclesiastical building in

[1] K. J. Conant, *The Apse at Cluny*. Speculum, volume VII. 1922. Page 23 et seq.

Northern France between the Abbey church of St. Denis (consecrated in 1144) and the burning of the old cathedral of Chartres in 1194, that is to say in the Early Gothic period (Senlis, Noyon [Fig. 9], Paris [Fig. 13], Mantes, Mouzon [where the original eastern end of the choir was derived from Laon], St. Rémi at Reims, Châlons-sur-Marne, Saint-Germain-des-Prés in Paris, St. Leu d'Esserent), there emerged as many different solutions as buildings. The type of ground plan might also be varied in details, as in the number of sides to the choir polygon, or in the choice between single and double aisled ambulatories, with or without chapels; but the enclosure of the inner choir in an "envelope" of space remained constant. Only in the cathedral of Laon was the ambulatory choir (without chapels), which existed to start with, replaced during the period of building by a plain enclosed choir adding length to the interior (Fig. 13 and Plate 52).

Chartres

The High Gothic classic cathedrals introduced many spatial features. The splendour of the chancel architecture was already foreshadowed in the form of the ground plan. Let us take Chartres as an example (Fig. 14). The nave and transepts have three aisles. The eastern end, majestically laid out with five aisles, extends so far that the transept withdraws, so to speak, into the middle of the cathedral. On the mean axis, beyond the eastern piers of the crossing, we pass through the long choir, at the farthest end of which an architectural structure in the form of a half rotunda spreads outwards in the shape of a fan (Fig. 21 and Plate 9). In the inner curve of the east end of the choir the great arcades rise above seven sides of a dodecagon. Behind them there runs a double ambulatory, forming an extension to the apse of the long choir, from the outer aisle of which open seven chapels, alternately deep and shallow in plan, and in which the width of the trapezoidal vault compartment over the ambulatories (separated by round pillars) varies correspondingly. The exceptionally intricate form of this ground plan implied that many problems, difficult to solve, were to be expected for the elevations. All those conditions applicable to the erection of the nave, with its two straight lines of wall and regular sequence of bays, were altered in the choir.

A vital question was the form of support in the apse. Of course the basic elevational system of the whole cathedral, with its straight sequence of bays, could be continued in the long choir. But at the far end the axial spacing for the ground-floor supports, and correspondingly for the vaulting

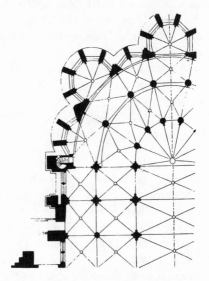

Fig. 21: CHARTRES. Plan of Choir

shafts above, contracts. As a result there is no room for the mighty compound piers of the master of Chartres or for his huge window groups.

The master, however, found an admirable architectural solution which unhappily cannot be appreciated at its full value today owing to eighteenth-century alterations to the choir arcades. He abandoned his compound pillar, choosing a round one and adorning it with a single shaft facing the nave. He then divided his four-arch triforium in half, allotting two arches to each narrow bay and piercing the wall above with five huge lancet windows, each forty-six feet in height from triforium to roof, the solemn monumental effect of which, with the enthroned Virgin in the centre, bathes the whole nave in glowing colours.

In order to be able to appreciate the technical achievement and the intellectual and practical capacity of an architect designing a Gothic cathedral, we must not forget that he was in no position to decide as he wished about the dimensions and organization of the ground plan. He had often to take into consideration what had occurred in earlier days on the same site. Thus Chartres Cathedral stands on the foundations of the early eleventh-century building burnt in 1194; similarly, for example, Strasbourg rose from the foundations of the building built by Bishop Werner during the Ottonian period. From the fire of the old cathedral of Chartres the crypt was preserved, a place hallowed as an ancient shrine to the Virgin. The cathedral, indeed, is built on a site with very old religious associations, which owed its importance to a spring with healing powers and to the cult of Our Saviour's Mother. We can still identify this place, if we descend to the crypt, where there is a chapel for the adoration of the Virgin Mary. This crypt stretches under the nave of the existing church as a very wide passage roofed with ribbed vaulting. The architect of the Gothic cathedral had to take all this into his calculations. He was able to make use of the foundations of the nave, and the building was, therefore, begun here; but for the transepts new footings had to be laid first, and for the complex plan of the choir, even though the old cathedral had an ambulatory and chapels, the foundation walls needed reinforcement. It was precisely this consideration for the three old chapels radiating in a wide arc from the ambulatory of the eleventh-century crypt which complicated the architect's task in achieving an architecturally harmonious solution for the Gothic choir to be erected above them. Viollet-le-Duc sharply criticized the architect's plan for the choir of Chartres (Dictionnaire 1, 235), stressing the irregularities of the construction, but without mentioning the difficulties to be overcome. G. Dehio, on the other hand, calls the choir of Chartres the "most beautiful of all Gothic choirs" (11, 126).

Because of the crypt chapels, the Gothic master varied the width of the ambulatory bays and of the spaces between the piers, as well as the extent of projection of the chapels. (The more deeply projecting stand over those built in the eleventh century.) A glance at the vault of the double ambulatories will make clear even to the layman how involved his task was. What emerged under these conditions, in association with the side aisles of the choir, was one of the most impressive achievements in the domain of Gothic cathedral interiors. The eye, differing in its view from the camera lens, sees

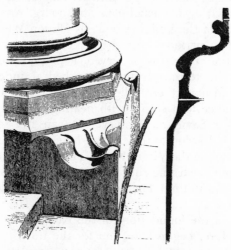

Fig. 22: CHARTRES. Pedestal in the Ambulatory

the axial spacing, exquisitely proportioned to their height, of the round piers set on massive bases (Fig. 22), the separation of inner and outer ambulatories by a continuous ribbon of steps (Plate 10) from which the great columns rise, the alternating rhythm of this succession of piers beginning with one of octagonal form, and finally the spatial link with the colonnade of the choir aisles. We could justifiably speak of the plastic modelling of the ambulatories.

The deeply projecting chevet chapels, each enclosed on five sides of an octagon, are separated from the ambulatory by cross arches, the "shallow" chapels are seemingly con-

tracted by the vault compartment and the associated bay
of the ambulatory. The chapel windows, glazed to their
full width, form an almost unbroken expanse of glowing
colour, which was also once the case in the choir of St. Denis.

Reims

A comparison between the architecture of the choirs of
Chartres and Reims provides the most explicit way to an
understanding of the architectural variety which was possible in similar spatial features of the great classic cathedrals.
At Reims, too, the choir is joined to a three-aisled transept
and has an ambulatory with chapels, although the plan is
much altered (Fig. 23). The inner polygon rises in a semi-
circle on five sides of a decagon, so that the lateral aisles
extend round the choir as a simple ambulatory with trapezoidal vault panels. Conforming to the five axes of the
polygon there is a garland of five chapels, identical in shape
and deeply projecting. The "five-tenths" vault compartment
at the eastern end of the choir is in the tradition of the Early
Gothic cathedral choir. We must examine and evaluate it
in its relation to the axial spacing of the piers, to the vault
of the choir, to the siting of the keystone and to the possibility of effecting a satisfactory junction with the straight
sides of the choir. The attempt was made to achieve as far
as possible a symmetrical and logical extension of the
elevational system round the semi-circle of the apse. There
were occasions when Early Gothic choirs did this with
astonishing skill by the use of the "five-tenths" vault.
At Reims itself the choir of St. Rémi (*circa* 1180) is an
important instance. Here the ground plan, with the advantage of an especially wide inner choir, shows how the
architect succeeded in maintaining the axial spacing of the
piers right round the choir and, in the process, continuing
the intricate elevational system in a uniform pattern to the
back of the high altar. The transition from the choir to the
semi-circle of the apse proceeds without any interruption,
indicating once more how much the use of the round pier
contributes to the desired effect. A symmetrical solution of

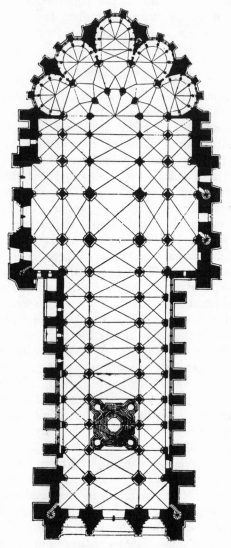

Fig. 25: REIMS Cathedral

this kind was impracticable in the classic cathedrals because of other dominating considerations and the requirements of the plan. Hence the "seven-twelfths" vault of Chartres is more sharply isolated from the choir as we have seen, thanks to a very different solution which uses contrast, rather than harmony, in the elevational design of the choir bays. Jean d'Orbais, on the other hand, who began the choir of Reims in 1212, aimed at harmony in the formal arrangement and a carefully balanced transition from the chevet to the choir, and thence to the architecture of the entire nave. He used the "five-tenths" vault panel in his design for the apse, adding a front compartment, so that the plan looks like an expanded version of St. Rémi. For the elevations he was able to extend to the semi-circle of the apse, despite the reduced width of the bays, his scheme for the straight walls of the choir in, so to speak, abridged form. He, too, was obliged to abandon the compound pier and, like the master of Chartres, chose the round pillar with a single vaulting shaft facing inwards, which establishes a vertical link with the wall above. The width of the triforium gallery is reduced by half, while the new creation of the tracery window permits the same arrangement of the clerestory for both the end of the choir and the nave. As a result the choir fits perfectly into the general pattern of the cathedral interior. The transition from the modest scale of the chevet to the greater dimensions of the transept is effected gradually by widening the axial spacing towards the west and by strengthening the compound piers.

The variety which is possible in handling the chevet chapels is apparent in a comparison with Chartres. At Reims the chapels, with their deeply extending interiors, are more completely isolated from each other and from the ambulatory. The architectural character of both plan and elevation is rooted in the customs of Champagne and is marked by elaborate composition (Plate 31). The circular plan is converted into a polygon above the socle and along this runs a passage, the wall below being adorned with a dummy arcade. The three sides facing outwards have the new tracery windows designed by the architect of Reims and previously

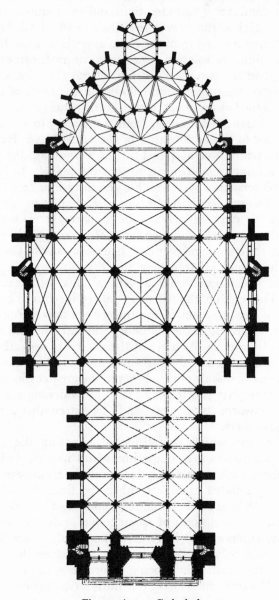

Fig. 24: AMIENS Cathedral

described, while those in the niche-like recesses of the closed sides assume the form of false arches. The architect uses compound piers to mark the line of separation from the ambulatory, and extends the moulding along the top of the socle to form a ring about the pier. The plain base rests upon an inclined skirting block, the capitals being decorated with delicate foliage, intermingled with figures (Fig. 25). Outside on the buttresses stand angels with outstretched wings, leading the choir of the angels, a theme which envelops the whole cathedral.

Fig. 25: Reims. Capital (Viollet-le-Duc)

Villard de Honnecourt drew both the interior and the exterior of the chapels with precision and included them as examples of fine architecture in his sketchbook.[1]

Amiens

Robert de Luzarches, who in 1220 began the nave of Amiens Cathedral, the third and largest of the three great Gothic cathedrals of France, developed a very high degree of symmetry in the disposition and relationship of all the features of the interior (Fig. 24). In his design, too, the eastern

[1] Cf. H. R. Hahnloser. *Villard de Honnecourt*. 1935. Plates 60 and 61.

end of the church opens out of three-aisled transepts to
form a choir surmounted by three oblong vault compart-
ments, with double ambulatories on each side (the aisle on
the outside being narrower than the inner one) (Fig. 26).
The polygon of the choir rises, as at Chartres, on seven sides
of a dodecagon; but, differing from Chartres and similar to
the plan of Jean d'Orbais, he chose a simple ambulatory,
from which seven chapels radiate, corresponding to the
axial layout of the polygon of the choir. In the elevational
arrangement of the apse he achieved the highest possible
harmony with the choir by retaining the basic form of the
compound pillar, in spite of the reduced axial spacing, and
by raising and narrowing the side arches more than was the
case at Reims. The "stilted" effect of the narrow arches at

Fig. 26: AMIENS. Section through the chancel (DURAND)

Fig. 27: AMIENS. Pier (choir)

the eastern end of the choir enhances the sharp verticality, characteristic of the architecture of Amiens Cathedral.

And now let us turn to the chevet chapels (Figs. 28 and 29). In comparison with architecture such as this, the chapels of Reims seem to return to the stylistic principles of Early Gothic, to a realm of graceful formal patterns, intimate in scale. At Amiens intimacy is completely rejected. Dimensions of majestic clarity, a disciplined and precise formal vocabulary, and an infallible sensibility in striking the exact note which turns architecture into music, leave no doubt that in the building of Robert de Luzarches the purest essence of Gothic found expression. On five sides of a polygon each chapel rises sheer. The structural scheme is deliberately, transparently, simple. Above the socle, ornamented with dummy arches, three tracery windows, set at an angle to one another, thrust upwards forty-six feet. The chapels are separated from the ambulatory by elegant clustered pillars

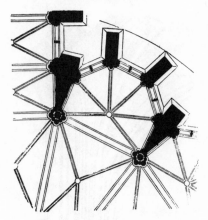

Fig. 28: AMIENS. Chevet chapel

(Fig. 29), their sculptural form developed from the round compound pier. Between the principal shafts, thinner columns are introduced with particularly happy effect. We can appreciate why the sublime architecture of the choir of Amiens was widely used as a model in France and indeed for Cologne Cathedral also.

3. THE TRANSEPTS

IN THE planning of the transepts Early Gothic ecclesiastical buildings do not by any means reveal an identical approach. Admittedly this feature was included between the nave and the choir in almost all the larger churches—among cathedrals, Bourges (Fig. 13), and, among Collegiate churches, Mantes, were notable exceptions—but the ground plan, siting, organization and method of enclosure vary from building to building. The three classic cathedrals of Chartres, Reims and Amiens placed three-aisled transepts in front of the choir, thus bisecting the church from north to south; and, in their exemplification of the great building principles of the early thirteenth century, exercised an enormous

Fig. 29: AMIENS. Chevet chapel (VIOLLET-LE-DUC)

influence on the effect created by the whole building. From the point of view of striving for symmetry in the interior, there are advantages in having no transept, which interrupts the formal continuity. But the cross arms make an extremely dramatic pause in the progress towards the sanctuary. In front of the Holy of Holies a huge boxlike space is constructed, which heightens still further the significance of the eastern part of the church and, as we look towards the high altar, makes an imposing meeting with the architecture of the high nave wall. In addition the transepts introduce special conditions which result from the intermediate position of the nave and choir, and from the external effect sought by the architect.

The Crossing

The place where the cross arms of the transepts bisect the main building is marked by piers which surpass in their monumental grandeur all other forms of support in the cathedral. Except at Reims, where the mouldings of the nave wall are extended round the crossing piers, four groups of shafts, rhythmically arranged according to thickness and symmetry, rise from base to abaci in unbroken lines towards the cross arches and intersecting ribs of the crossing vault (Plate 9). Thus the structural centre of the cathedral opens giant gateways to the four realms of heaven—the nave, the two arms of the transepts and the choir. As we look from the nave, the eastern crossing piers stand like huge dark wings before the entrance to the brilliantly lighted choir, heightening the impression of the boxlike character of the transepts.

In early days this effect was enhanced by the rood-screen which was placed in front of the eastern pillars of the crossing and which segregated the choir from the transepts. Chartres used to have a screen richly ornamented with sculpture, which initiated a new High Gothic type (Fig. 30).[1] Erected about 1230 (destroyed in 1763), it consisted of a stage or loft more than sixty feet wide, resting upon a solid

[1] H. Bunjes, *Der gotische Lettner der Kathedrale von Chartres*. Wallraf-Richartz-Jahrbuch XII/XIII. 1943. Page 70 et seq.
  Erika Kirchner-Doberer, *Die deutschen Lettner bis 1300*. Wiener Dissertation, 1946.

Fig. 30: Original rood-screen of CHARTRES Cathedral

partition on the choir side (with access through the middle) and in front upon an arcade of seven arches. The full height of the screen was about twenty-five feet, and a fairly accurate idea of its architecture can be obtained from old descriptions, pictures and fragments. The ornamental sculpture with, as its principal theme, scenes from the Life of Our Lord, is artistically important and has survived in part, being preserved in the crypt. A relief depicting the Evangelists is in the Louvre.

Amiens Cathedral also had a screen of the Chartres type, but it is known to us only from documents and old drawings.

With regard to the architecture of the transepts of Chartres, the stately disposition of the nave is preserved for both the east and west walls, as indeed we should expect from the building's all pervading spirit of uniformity. There is, however, a hardly detectable difference. The triforium, owing to special structural conditions, is composed of five sections in the transepts instead of the four used in the nave, and the arches are rather more pointed. In consequence, the triforium appears as a more sharply defined continuous horizontal band, separating ground and clerestories, than is the case in the nave.

The Rose

The two façade walls of the transepts have a place of special significance, because the elevational system of the nave is not extended to them. They have their own architectural form. If we pause beneath the crossing of Chartres Cathedral and look north, west and south, we see the great rose windows flooding the walls in glowing colours.

In the mediaeval art of church building the architecture of windows played its most important rôle in the classic phase of Gothic, in which the master of Chartres was supreme, as we have already seen from an analysis of his composite windows in the nave. His place in art history, however, must once again be stressed in relation to the magnificent conception of the rose window. At Chartres the rose, the principal window feature, dominates the whole range of windows in the clerestories of the nave (Plate 1) and transepts, but is not used in the choir. This splendid feature is found first in the rose of the west front, an example of architectural embellishment of surpassing beauty. An earlier instance is to be found in the transept rose of Laon Cathedral, which repeats the circle theme of the whole window in the design itself. The rose of Laon, like the west rose of Chartres, is constructed with pierced stone panels and at Chartres solid stone is almost completely eliminated. At Laon there are eight principal openings and twelve at Chartres. About this inner circle a wreath of twelve mullions is arranged like spokes, radiating outwards to twelve small circular windows. The design appealed so much to Villard de Honnecourt that he included this "ronde verrière" in his sketchbook, giving it incidentally a still more elaborate pattern in certain respects.[1] What does not fully appear in his drawing is the decorative effect of the whole, which is worthy of a goldsmith, especially in the external architecture. This impression is not only determined by the harmonious relationship of all the openings to one another and by an air of unfolding from the centre outwards, but by vigorous modelling and deeply incised relief carving. The circles are no mere empty forms, but are executed with small sharply recessed arcs, the large central circle having twelve, the smaller external ones eight such "foils". In addition the inner rims of the circles are adorned with little flowering roses. Even the little quatrefoil openings on the outer edge have rosettes on the mouldings, while the arches in the middle are plain.

The great rose windows of the cathedrals each have two very different aspects, depending upon whether they are seen from inside or outside. Externally their architectural composition is decided by the design of the building as a whole. Internally they form only a dark framework for the vibrant glow of the stained glass, flooding the cathedral interior with a mystical blaze of colour.

The transept rose windows of Chartres (Plate 3) are superimposed on five lancets, as in the north transept façade of Laon, but at Laon the transept wall is deeply recessed, since the lateral aisles and tribune galleries are continued round it. The transept roses at Chartres have tracery stonework and harmonize with the elevational design of the nave to the extent that they transfer the form of the composite window (rose with lancets) to the huge dimensions of the transept façades, and occupy the full width of these walls.

The majestic rose windows of the north and south fronts also provide the transept interiors of the classic cathedrals with their most important visual features by far, but the pattern of the tracery and the extent to which the wall is

[1] Hahnloser, *Villard de Honnecourt*. Plate 30.

pierced vary. In Reims Cathedral the entire wall was translucent, thanks to the circumstance that the transept façades had no portals. The balance of the design for the north wall is destroyed by the portal constructed later, but on the south side its true qualities can still be appreciated. The whole wall is of double thickness and is breached from the socle to the base of the triforium by a group of three high windows, with a passage in front which runs round the entire cathedral (Plate 28). The triforium area of the transept, of double thickness also, is breached by three oculi associated with an arcade. The rose is suspended above. While the rose windows of the transept at Chartres fit closely into the round arch of the outer wall, exactly like the roses of the clerestory in the nave, the transept roses at Reims, in deference to the tracery construction, are more loosely related to the construction. For the first time the circle of the rose is placed beneath a pointed arch, so that the wall surface is pierced between the crown of the rose window and the containing arch.

A later development is shown in the transept façades of the cathedral of Notre-Dame in Paris and the Abbey church of St. Denis. In Paris, the very skilfully composed rose windows are inlaid in a square, in which the lower spandrels are adorned with tracery.

The interior side of the west wall at Reims (Plate 32) offers a highly individual, extremely elaborate and, indeed, apparently unique composition. The great rose window under a pointed-arch vault is associated here with a continuous gallery; while, below it, the tympanum of the arch of the main portal is filled with a second rose. Framing this arch from top to bottom, the wall consists of seven tiers of niches, each containing a statue depicting a character from the Bible.

The cross arms of Amiens Cathedral also have a rose window in the upper part of the façade walls, which is combined with a fenestrated triforium to provide a translucent surface extending to the full width of the wall. The tracery of these roses, however, belongs to a later period (fourteenth and sixteenth centuries).

4. LIGHT

UNTIL NOW we have only examined the carcase of the Gothic wall in the nave, choir and transepts. This alone is not enough to determine the particular quality of the cathedral interior. We must consider a further element, which is of decisive importance in the effect created by a Gothic cathedral: light.

The Mystical Power of Light

The window openings of mediaeval churches are largely judged by the amount of light which they allow inside. But this overlooks the real significance of the church interior, which is not concerned with differences of degree in holiness but with light as a spiritual power, capable of exercising an influence as inspiring as architectural form. In the dark barrel-vaulted churches of the twelfth century, which probably welcomed the faithful only with candles, there reigned a religious atmosphere very different from that which prevailed in thirteenth-century churches flooded with coloured light. The luminous Gothic interior contrasts strongly, moreover, with, on the one hand, the crypt-like gloom of, in particular, the round vaulted Romanesque churches of Auvergne, Provence, Poitou, the great Pilgrimage churches like St. Sernin at Toulouse or Santiago de Compostela, and, on the other, with the bright naturally lit churches of the Renaissance. We must, therefore, try to understand more exactly the real nature of light in the Gothic cathedral. There is also the problem of differentiating between styles of light, just as we distinguish between styles of architecture, and this is something which has hardly been considered in relation to Western ecclesiastical art. The direction by which light enters leads to considerable variations. We know how different is the effect produced in a hall church with three high aisles, in which the light enters through the external walls of the lateral aisles, or in an interior of basilical section, in which the light is concentrated in the upper part of the nave and also provides strong illumination in the clerestory of the choir. We recall—by way of indicating the possibilities of light in its effect on internal space—the interior of the Pantheon in Rome with its circular opening in the crown of the dome, or the Late Gothic architect Hans Stethaimer, who successfully combined the different features of two building styles in the Franciscan church at Salzburg, investing the altar of the Virgin in an aura of sublime reverence with the aid of contrasting styles of light.

For an understanding of the mystical light of the middle ages we shall not obtain much help by referring to the metaphysics of light, which derived from St. Augustine and had a prominent place in mediaeval theology. The question as to "whether and how far the mediaeval metaphysics of light can help to elucidate the meaning of the obviously deliberate luminosity in mediaeval painting" has been comprehensively treated by Wolfgang Schöne, so that we can turn to his exposition here.[1]

It is difficult to imagine any direct influence of the theological idea of light on the origin of a new ecclesiastical style like Gothic, since metaphysical light does not belong to the realm of the senses, but is of the mind, bringing the intangible nature of God closer to the religious conception. "The language of art does not speak the language of speculation, which can distinguish between the light of the senses and the light of the mind, but has, so to speak only one word for 'light'. The speculative conception of light must try to bridge visual and intellectual realities and experiences logically, while in the vocabulary of art both are one. While mediaeval painting left out shade it raised visible light to the power of a super-sensual light; for all sensual or natural light gives shade. In all this it cannot be too strongly emphasized that in mediaeval thought, because of its theological basis, the

[1] Wolfgang Schöne, *Über das Licht in der Malerei*. Berlin, 1954. Page 55 et seq.

view of a work of art 'as such' is rejected."[1] This attitude applies equally to the light of the Gothic interior.

Gothic Light

The story of light in mediaeval places of worship makes it quite clear that its particular character was directly related to architectural form. In the classic Gothic cathedrals its quality, abundance and distribution contributed decisively to the design of the interior. Unfortunately Gothic light has rarely survived in its pure form, since the windows of most churches have lost their original decorative glazing or contain only fragments of the early glass. The effect is not the same when a thirteenth-century interior is filled with fourteenth- or fifteenth-century light, for Gothic light changed its style in the character of the colour.

If we want to understand the grandeur of cathedral light as it was known to the thirteenth century, we must first turn to Chartres, the sole instance of a High Gothic cathedral which still preserves the original light as a whole (with the exception of a few windows) from the period when the cathedral was built. Besides Chartres, the choirs of Beauvais, Le Mans and Bourges deserve mention. They reveal, firstly, that Gothic light is not a "natural" light and, secondly, that this "unnaturalness", when experienced in conjunction with the inspiring power of the architecture, becomes a "supernatural" light. The Gothic interior is bathed in a dark, reddish violet light, which has a mysterious quality difficult to describe, and which, in particular, does not come from a single source, seeming to fluctuate in its brightness according to the weather of the natural world outside, now swelling, now receding, now filling the twilit colours with an unimaginable incandescence. That this is no transparent light, but that the windows themselves are its source, has been stressed by Wolfgang Schöne, who describes the light of the stained-glass windows as "combining an artificial light of their own

---

[1] Schöne, page 70. Otto v. Simson (*The Gothic Cathedral*, London and New York, 1956) has tried to indicate the influence of the Augustinian metaphysics of light on the original conception of the Gothic cathedral.

developed to the highest possible intensity with colour developed to the highest possible intensity (darkness, brilliance, depth)".[1]

In some respects this light takes the place of architecture under certain conditions. Anybody who has seen Chartres Cathedral without its stained glass[2]—in a natural light, that is to say—will grasp this at once. The coloured light softens the sinewy lines of the architectural framework until it merges into a physically solid structure, in which architecture and coloured light make the containing sides of the lofty nave into a luminous wall. For, until Chartres was built, with its new design of clerestory, windows had never been extended to such a width to form panels of coloured light filling the entire wall. With the coloured light acting as an essential element in the containment of space, the mystical enchantment of thirteenth-century interiors became an architectural expression of a sense of complete escape from workaday environment, a feeling of having "overcome the world" of material things.

The importance of light in the design of the cathedral interior, so far as its real nature is concerned, is only partly understood. The "unnatural" Gothic light confronts us also with a pictorial world of the richest imagery, its silent power exercising enormous influence over mankind. But reference to this world of pictorial allegory and symbolism must be reserved for a special chapter.

5. Gothic Space and its Containment

IN CONSIDERING theories about style, little has so far been said about the nature of Gothic space and its containment. The first problem is to decide whether, as a general principle, we should apply to it the ambiguous conception of a room in the architectural sense. Those whose ideas have been formed

---

[1] Schöne, *Über das Licht in der Malerei.* 1954. Page 38.
[2] The glass was removed during the war.

by the Renaissance will certainly say "No". The architectural historian, who has also probably been nurtured on the
Renaissance or on classicism, regards a "room" as a boxlike
structure, bounded on all sides by solid enclosing walls.
This is clearly not the case in the Gothic cathedral, in which
(as originally conceived) the enclosing walls appear diaphanous, intangible, luminous, like the golden background
in mediaeval painting. In point of fact we cannot point to
any particular characteristic which distinguishes such spatial
qualities from those of any other form of enclosed space. We
cannot speak of "spacelessness", for no matter how we look
at it, the cathedral interior remains a space through which
one can pass. We have, therefore, to try to identify other
distinctive features of the Gothic interior.

Once again we must turn to the upper nave wall and
examine its structure, for from it the special nature of the
interior is derived. And what, we may ask, is so particularly
Gothic in the Gothic way of containing space? The answer
is: just so little as there is of natural light in the cathedral,
just so little is there of "natural" antagonism between support
and load in the architecture of the elements enclosing the
interior. What is meant by the antagonism between support
and load is most clearly shown by the temple architecture of
ancient Greece. The architectural elements of post and
beam provide visible evidence that with stone the law of
gravity prevails. The columns of classical times were of load-
bearing stone. Greek architecture was based upon the law of
gravity or weight.

Weightlessness

This is not the case with Gothic. On the contrary, Gothic
church architecture wages an incessant war against weight.
It rejects it in order to create a place of enchantment, a space
transcending earthly experience.

How does Gothic architecture achieve this effect? How
was it possible in the process of construction to circumvent
the natural conflict between support and load, which the
law of gravity imposes? This law cannot be cancelled out,
for Gothic cathedrals are built of stone.

Verticality

In the Gothic nave wall there is no hint of load bearing. All its characteristics are essentially vertical. The vault is not felt as something heavy, hardly indeed as a cover, but simply as the place towards which the lines of upward thrust converge. This intrinsic peculiarity can be explained by the concept of verticality in which we must distinguish between verticality as spatial proportion and verticality as a principle of elevational design.

Verticality as spatial proportion is not confined to Gothic, but has existed in Western ecclesiastical architecture since Charlemagne. The Palatinate chapel at Aix-la-Chapelle is emphatically vertical in conception. The Carolingian West Gothic churches of Asturias in Northern Spain exemplify in certain instances a straight-up, shaftlike interpretation of space. The majestic Abbey church of Cluny, with its pointed-arch vault, is surprisingly vertical in its proportions, as can still be appreciated in the transept arm which survived the destruction. The cathedral of St. Lazare at Autun demonstrates similar spatial relationships applied to another large building in twelfth-century Burgundy. The same thing occurs in Provence, where the dark barrel-vaulted interiors, with their narrow lateral aisles, rise to astonishing heights in proportion to their superficial area.

In comparison, the Early Gothic cathedrals of Northern France are very restrained. The proportions of the interior do not depend for their effect exclusively on an absolute relationship between breadth and height. No particular impression of verticality can be discerned in the form of the interior of Laon Cathedral. This is because in the design of the high nave wall continuous horizontal formal features counteract the verticals.

In buildings of the classic cathedral type—Chartres, Reims, Amiens—spatial proportions and principles of elevational design combine to achieve that emphatic Gothic verticality, and forestall from the first any impression of heaviness.

The steady increase in the internal height of the naves of the cathedrals of Chartres (120 feet), Reims (125 feet),

Amiens (138 feet) particularly favoured this development. In the Gothic choirs of Beauvais (Fig. 39) and Le Mans these dimensions were even exceeded, and at Beauvais the vault collapsed. The demands in fact were too much for the technical resources. Dehio called this episode "the Icarus flight of Gothic". The phenomenon of these interiors—first and best exemplified by Amiens Cathedral—was described by Worringer as "vertical ecstasy".

Invisible Support

The impression of a weightless wall soaring above the nave is heightened by the lack of any visible feature in the interior technically capable of holding a structure of this kind upright. Why doesn't it tilt over? Why doesn't it collapse, in view of the number and extent of the perforations? The cardinal principle of Gothic wall construction lay in disposing externally (and out of sight from the interior) the technical means for supporting it. What these technical means looked like must be discussed in detail later.

Diaphanous Structure

A further opportunity for diminishing the character of weight in the impression given by the upper nave wall, without completely "dematerializing" it, lay in the manner in which it is placed in a transparent spatial setting. This is the phenomenon which I have described, in order to illustrate the underlying Gothic principle, as "diaphanous structure". It also formed the substance of certain observations of mine in a paper read in 1927 to the Freiburg Scientific Society "On the Gothic church interior".

First a word must be said about the containment of space in High Gothic church building. In the basilical section of a structure with several aisles the material limits of the ground floor are set by the external walls of the lateral aisles, but these limits are not always identical with those which are effective in conveying the feeling of space, any more than they are necessarily identified with one particular layer of wall. In the cathedral the nave, over its entire length as far as, and including, the high altar, conveys this feeling of space. Every development is related to the nave, the cardinal space of Gothic church building, and its limits, which we are discussing here, are fixed by the upper nave wall. The relationship of the subsidiary spaces to the nave, whether aisles, ambulatories or galleries, can be analysed from various points of view. We shall consider them here as enveloping the upper nave wall in a mantle of space. In the "diaphanous structure" of the Gothic system of enclosing space we are concerned with a visual relationship between the plastically modelled wall and the "subsidiary spaces" behind it. We must recognize as well that this relationship does not apply to every kind of wall opening and that it does not depend on the fortuitous size of the opening. Romanesque, too, reveals very extensive openings in the enclosing walls of the nave, but without the quality of a "diaphanous structure". In the early twelfth century pilgrimage churches of the type of St. Sernin in Toulouse or Conques, wide arcade and tribune gallery openings stand one above the other. But the dominant conception of the wall is of a broad expanse of masonry, the keynote of which is uninterrupted solidity. This conception of the continuous wall is most clearly exemplified in eleventh-century buildings, such as Vignory or similar structures, in which the upper nave wall is an unbroken plain surface. The wall, however, can be enlivened by stepping the arcades, by tribune galleries or by projections associated with the arches for the barrel-vault, without disturbing the impression of continuous mass, for all such elements are "extruded" from the wall face. The openings are merely intervals in a continuous mass of masonry, so that the basis of the design of the nave wall of a Romanesque church can be considered as an alternation of open and closed panels, even when these only consist of piers to represent the continuous nature of the wall.

The Gothic wall is very different in structure. It is not enough to say that it is pierced to the ultimate possible degree. The Gothic nave wall is not distinguished from its Romanesque counterpart by having more openings, but by a visually different relationship to the "subsidiary spaces". It rejects the characteristic of continuous mass, to the extent that it is entirely composed of plastically modelled, cylindrical elements. One glance at the upper nave wall of Laon Cathedral will be enough to understand what is meant. At ground level the cylindrically shaped piers are the dominant feature, and in the tribunes and triforium it is the slim, round colonnettes of the linked arches. Circular vaulting shafts climb to the full height of the nave wall in clusters and merge into the curved ribs of the vault. The mouldings of the side arches and those at the base of the tribunes, triforium and clerestory windows are all in the form of round bars. In short, the architecture of the Gothic wall cannot be understood as continuous mass, but as plastic modelling.

In this respect it achieves a new relationship with the multifarious layers of space lying behind it. "Diaphanous structure" implies that the modelling of the wall is a form of architectural relief projecting from a background of space and that the latter determines the Gothic character of this method of space-containment. The Gothic wall is not to be understood without this spatial background acting as a foil, and its effect on the whole of the cathedral interior is obtained only in this way. The archways of the great arcades, of course, provide access to the aisles from the nave, but this has nothing to do with the visual relationship between nave and aisles. In a work of art, and therefore in a masterwork of architecture, every feature can combine in itself different degrees of significance and relationship, which attain their full value by the manner in which they are associated with other forms. We must also take the following into account with respect to "diaphanous structure".

Spatial Background and Plastic Modelling of the Wall

1. The entire expanse of wall is set against a background of space, which is either in darkness or consists of coloured light, so that the nave of the Gothic cathedral appears to be enclosed in an envelope of space.
2. The effect of the background of space and of the plastic

modelling of the wall is complementary. This is not the case with the Romanesque wall, in which all features are subservient to the effects of continuous mass. The wall becomes Gothic as soon as the "round" modelling of the wall framework creates the character of a foil in the spatial elements lying behind it. The rounded piers at ground level and the cylindrical forms of the tribunes, triforium and vaulting shafts counteract the impression of massiveness. Since, moreover, the roundness stands out from the dark layer of space like sculptured form—the original light conditions, as at Chartres for example, are assumed—the "ground" also appears as such, thanks to the modelling. The nave wall looks like latticework placed in front of an envelope of space.

In conveying the spatial character of French Gothic, the principle of the diaphanous wall structure seems more expressive than particular details of form, more significant than the use of pointed arches and the cross-ribbed vault. That can easily be appreciated by looking at buildings which use pointed arches and the cross-ribbed vault in construction, but do not treat the wall in accordance with the principle of "diaphanous structure". Anyone who has been in the cathedral at Langres will recall that the interior is far from typically Gothic. The anti-Gothic effect of this building is expressed in the handling of the wall, which is conceived as a homogeneous mass.

In the strongest contrast to this is the "diaphanous structural" treatment of the nave walls of Laon Cathedral, or the southern transept arm of the cathedral of Soissons (to name Early Gothic examples), which do not rely on the cross-ribbed vault and pointed arches to determine their Gothic character. In the High Gothic cathedrals the interior acquires its character by this means.

The nave is wrapped in an envelope of space of various layers, the lateral aisles having a tendency to subordinate themselves completely to the nave. At Chartres, under certain conditions, they appear only as a dark ground.

At Reims the double thickness of the construction and wide window openings of the external walls of the aisles make them seem like a coloured light background to the nave wall. At Amiens it is clear that, because of the aisle chapels placed between the buttress piers, the spatial and visual conditions of a High Gothic basilica are substantially altered, all the more so since the original stained glass has been lost. For this reason it is difficult to appreciate the original impression created by the cathedral interior.

For the triforium the classic cathedral devised a form which made it possible to place along the nave wall, between the arcades and clerestory, a layer of space behind a lattice screen. By this means the triforium first appeared as a dark lining and finally in the choir of Amiens in a new form as a coloured light ground.

The clerestory above, which is preserved in its thirteenth-century form only at Chartres, appears as a coloured spatial layer enclosing the principal internal space of the nave.

The effect of the "diaphanous structure" as a further means of removing any impression of heaviness from the cathedral interior is most noticeable in the High Gothic architecture of the choir. The ambulatory, so characteristic of the form of French choirs, becomes in Gothic a shell of space round the sanctuary, providing as far as possible a light ground of uninterrupted colour for the choir arcade.

Above, the lattice-like wall of the apse is lined from top to bottom with strips of coloured light and dark ground.

The ultimate refinement of this principle was applied in certain French cathedral choirs, which exploit further than Chartres, Reims and Amiens, and by the boldest use of Gothic methods of construction, the system of contriving a background of space. At Beauvais the spatial shell of the ambulatory is associated with the increasing vertical emphasis of the soaring interior, now nearly 160 feet high, and is provided with its own triforium and series of windows. Beginning with the ambulatory and looking from the bottom upwards, we have the coloured light ground of the chapel windows, triforium and clerestory (which seem to be visually and formally associated with the arcades), and above these the triforium and clerestory of the nave wall.

The significance of the lateral aisle as a spatial foil for the main internal area is nowhere more clearly revealed than in the five-aisled plan of Le Mans, for it is quite impossible not to notice that the whole spatial composition, like the form of the space-containing structure itself, derives its meaning only from the space in the middle. The individual areas of background are distributed over various layers of space, so that the first aisle in relation to the second repeats the basilical motif of the principal internal area. Here, too, as at Beauvais coloured bands of light alternate with a dark spatial ground, and this stepped effect (which implies at the same time a stepping in depth and which is projected with its visual values, so to speak, on to the containing structure) is heightened by the vertical emphasis of the design, so that the light grows in intensity as it moves upwards and reveals its most expressive powers in the coloured imagery of the upper windows of the choir.

Only in one cathedral do we find this form of spatial composition realized for the entire nave: Bourges (Figs. 13 and 31). Although the long delays in completing the building led to changes in details, the original conception of the interior has survived through these and other vicissitudes. Here the Gothic theory of space—so far as the principle of "diaphanous structure" is concerned—enjoyed its most impressive realization, in which, thanks in particular to the absence of a transept, the interior displays the most remarkable unity.

We could object that the relationship of the nave wall to the aisles as one of relief to background can easily be seen in Early Gothic buildings, for here the arcades of the lowest storey are kept comparatively low and the connection with the lattice pattern of the upper nave wall is already apparent in the use of the quadripartite system. This does not apply to the three-tier scheme of High Gothic cathedrals, mainly because the greater height of the arcades and the open view which they offer into the aisles diminish the visual connection between the architecture of the arcades and the upper wall of the nave. This objection must be mentioned because of a theory which judges the Gothic church (and considers its historical development), so far as its spatial nature is concerned, as an endeavour to achieve a merging of every element of space (Paul Frankl, *Wölfflin-Festschrift*, 1924,

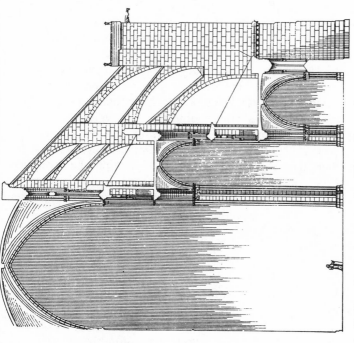

Fig. 31: BOURGES Cathedral. Longitudinal section and cross-section (DEHIO-BEZOLD)

p. 109). This theory implies that the nave and aisles inter-
mingle as a single spatial area, in which the piercing of the
upper nave wall is regarded as a means of uniting and pene-
trating space. This supposition, however, is invalid for
twelfth- and thirteenth-century Gothic in Northern France.
The increasing perforation of the nave wall and widening of
the arcades brought no sign of any closer connection between
the spatial elements lying behind the nave wall and the nave
itself. On the contrary a fascinating problem of Gothic
architecture lay in finding means, despite the ever-increasing
number of openings in the wall, of making the structure
enclosing the nave into a self-contained and self-complete
lattice screen. The use of the compound round pier, with its
projections and connections with the upper levels of the wall,
played an important visual rôle in this. It must also not be
overlooked that as the eye moves up the interior, the rows
of piers draw closer together because of foreshortening in
perspective.

This even holds good for a majestic five-aisled layout like
Bourges (Fig. 31), where the nave is girdled by two layers of
space. In spite of the high arcade openings in the containing
wall no merging occurs between nave and aisles. In relation
to the nave, the aisles remain mere shells, optical foils.
Perhaps this may be difficult to accept. We must, however,
imagine the original coloured light, which is still preserved
in the choir, distributed throughout the whole building and
forget all the later additions, in order to understand the idea
of a layer of space acting as a foil to the nave wall, in the
sense implied by "diaphanous structure".

6. On The Technique of The Cathedral

THE GOTHIC CATHEDRAL is a marvel of mediaeval technical
skill and craftsmanship. A mistaken nineteenth-century
view was that the cathedral was simply the result of progressive improvements in vault construction. Even Dehio

expressed the opinion that Gothic architecture grew out of a technical problem, while H. Focillon, in his fine book *Art d'Occident* (1938), begins the section on Gothic with a searching analysis of the origins of the ribbed vault. It was not appreciated that the architectural idea of the cathedral, inspired by the religious power of the time, could only be put into practice with the help of a most comprehensively considered technique. From the first this was no rigid system, but one which underwent modifications according to the problems posed by changes in the dimensions of the building, in its plan and section, and by the materials available. It may be observed that, in Early Gothic, technique sometimes lagged behind theory. The buildings of the period of the classic cathedrals were alone in being cast, technically and architecturally, from a single mould. That Gothic architects, at least the leaders among them, solved their technical problems is clearly proved by the cathedrals which, erected in a spirit of matchless structural daring, have survived through the centuries and have been threatened more by mankind's destructive spiritual crises than by inadequate technical knowledge or building failure, even if the effects of weathering have always demanded scrupulous care of the fabric with its brittle ornamentation. Of course, the technique had limitations. The twin towers of Laon Cathedral, too heavy for the transepts, and the collapse of the choir roof at Beauvais are familiar examples. Gothic architects were not engineers, but artists, who gave form to new ideas and sometimes demanded too much of their technique.

Site Organization

We must now take a look at the building site and its workshops, which were the sources of all technical experience. The time occupied in building these great churches, extending far beyond one man's life span, demanded an organization in which management, planning and supervision were co-ordinated and work space provided for the stonemason and sculptor. Of the cathedral of Chartres we know that the period spent in erecting the carcase of the building—begun in 1194, nave roof completed in 1220—was one of the shortest on record. In the case of Reims, begun in 1211, constructional work on the cathedral was still proceeding until the fifteenth century. The foundation stone of Notre-Dame in Paris was laid in 1163. The building of the choir, the first part of the church to be constructed, took about twenty years. The nave occupied a further two decades. The west front belongs essentially to the thirteenth century, the rose-window stage taking from about 1220 to 1225. Work on the towers, which remained without spires, lasted till about 1245. During the years after the mid-century the transepts acquired the new façades of Jean de Chelles. Roughly the same time was needed for building Laon Cathedral.

We know very little about Gothic site organization in the twelfth and thirteenth centuries or of the preliminaries to building. Most of our information comes from the late middle ages.[1] For the smaller thirteenth-century buildings we must also take into consideration the itinerant bands of building craftsmen, who can be traced in many instances from stylistic resemblances between churches or from the repetition of the same mason's marks. In the case of the large buildings, however, there was a combined and permanent planning office and workshop throughout the period of building. In the middle ages these site operations were known as "opus", the fabric, or simply the works (l'oeuvre). Job management and architects' work were regarded as separate activities. The job manager, who had to look after the business side, was called "operarius", while the architect in charge, or master of the works, was described as "magister operis".[2] A strong sense of brotherhood united master masons, journeymen, artisans and apprentice craftsmen, who were picked men with an acute sense of professional pride, as the records of the masons' lodges of the late middle ages bear witness.

[1] Cf. Pierre du Colombier, *Les Chantiers des Cathédrales*. Paris, 1953.
Paul Booz, *Der Baumeister der Gotik*. Munich-Berlin, 1956.
[2] Cf. Booz. Page 25.

1. CHARTRES cathedral. View of the nave wall from the south aisle

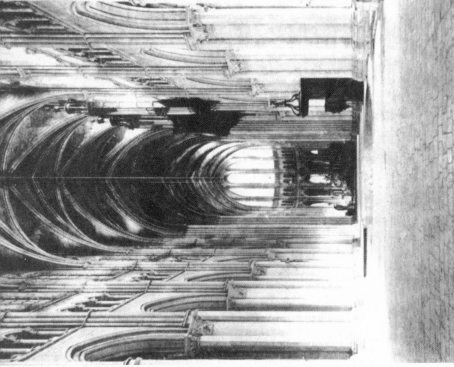

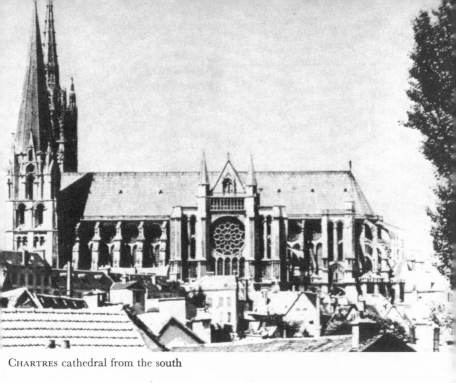

Chartres cathedral from the south

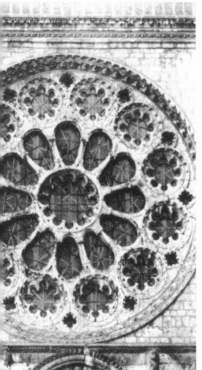

Chartres. The west rose

6. Chartres. Buttresses

7. CHARTRES. Nave vaulting

8. CHARTRES. Vaulting over the ambulatory

10. CHARTRES. Ambulatory

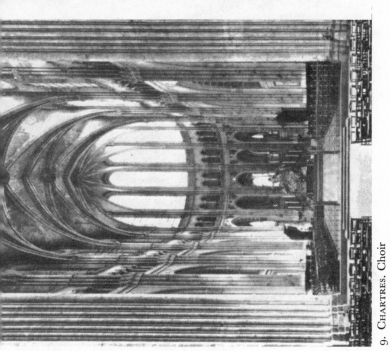

9. CHARTRES. Choir

11. CHARTRES. West portal (portail royal)

12. CHARTRES. West portal. Tympanum with Christ in His Glory, surrou
by the Evangelistic symbols

14. CHARTRES. West portal: the Seven Liberal Arts (detail)

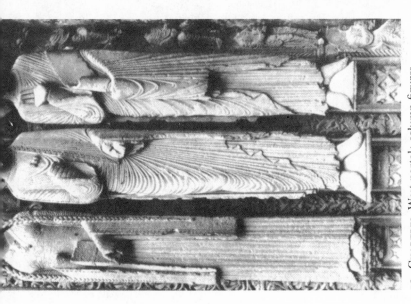

13. CHARTRES. West portal: column figures

15. CHARTRES. North transept porches

16. CHARTRES. Coronation, Death and Assumption of Mary

17. CHARTRES. Prophets of the Virgin por
Right to left: David, Samuel, Moses, Abraha
Melchisedek

18. CHARTRES. Mary and
Elizabeth (the Visitation)

19. CHARTRES. Left to right: Balaam,
the Queen of Sheba, Solomon

20. CHARTRES. Tobias with Sarah's father

21. CHARTRES. Judith strews her
head with ashes

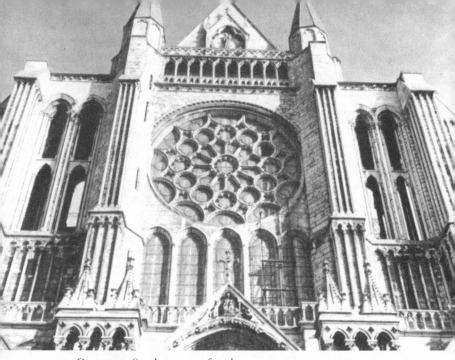

22. CHARTRES. South transept façade

23. CHARTRES. South transept porches

CHARTRES. The Last Judgment—middle portal of the south transept

CHARTRES.
ṛist—middle
tal of the south
ṣept

26. CHARTRES. Apostles—middle portal of the south transept

27. REIMS cathedral. Nave, looking east

28. REIMS. Transept

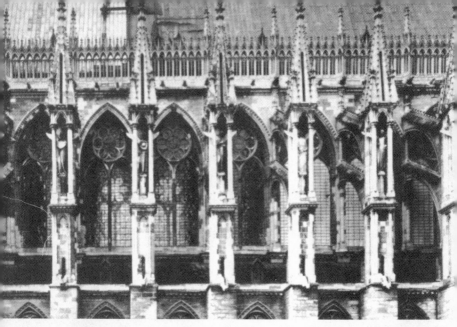

29. REIMS. Buttresses

30. REIMS. South aisle

31. REIMS. Chevet chapels

2. REIMS. West door (from inside)

33. REIMS. The Last Judgment—north transept

Top) REIMS. Christ sits in Judgment with Mary and John. Below, the dead rising
Middle) REIMS. The righteous are gathered into Abraham's bosom
Bottom) REIMS. The damned are led down into hell

37. REIMS. St. Peter   38. REIMS. Christ   39. REIMS. St. Paul

41. Reims. St. Paul

40. Reims. St. Peter

42. REIMS. West portal

44. REIMS. West portal. Left to right: the Angel of the Annunciation and Mary, Mary and Elizabeth, David, Solomon

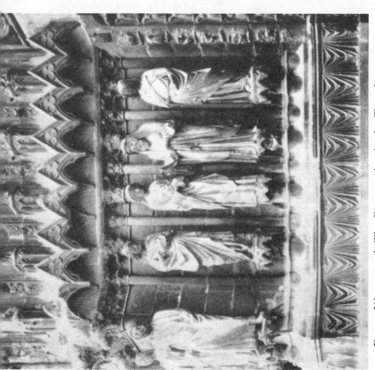

43. REIMS. West portal. The Presentation in the Temple

45. REIMS. The Annunciation

46. REIMS. Mary and Elizabeth (the Visitatic

47. REIMS. The Angel of the Annunciation

48. REIMS. Mary (from the Visitatic

49. REIMS. The Presentation in the Temple (Joseph, Mary with the Child, Simeon, Hanna)

50. REIMS. Saints' (Martyrs') Portal—north transept, known as the Sixtus
On the tympanum, stories from the lives of St. Sixte and St. Rémi

51. REIMS. West portal. St. Nicaise with two angels

54. AMIENS cathedral. Nave, looking east

55. AMIENS cathedral from the south-west

56. AMIENS. West portal

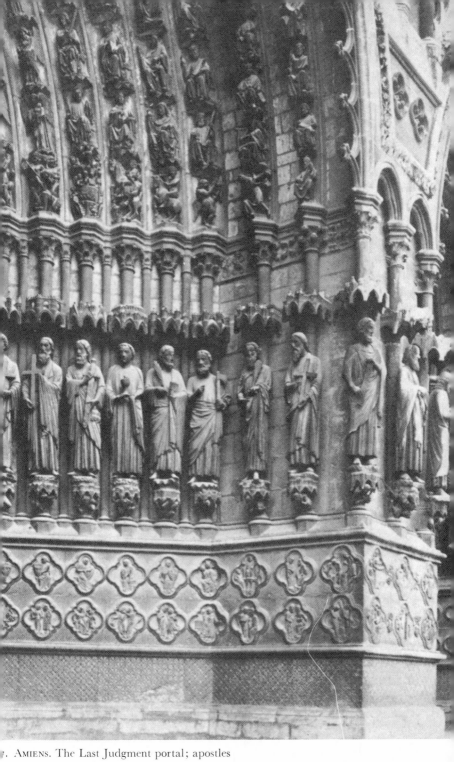

7. AMIENS. The Last Judgment portal; apostles

58. AMIENS. Virgin portal. Right to left: the Three

59. AMIENS. The Annunciation and Visitation

). Amiens. Middle portal. The Last Judgment (detail)

. Amiens. Middle portal. Christ   62. Chartres. Head of Christ

The Masters

We know some of the names of the leading architects, who designed the great thirteenth-century cathedrals in Northern France during the golden age of Gothic, but we know nothing of their personal lives.

The master builders of the classic cathedrals used a singularly imposing form of signature to record their contribution to the joint achievement. This takes the form of a "Labyrinth" inlaid in the floor of the nave, the one at Chartres (Fig. 32) occupying the entire width. At Reims

Fig. 32; CHARTRES, Labyrinth

and Amiens the labyrinths have not been preserved, but we know them from old drawings and documents, together with their inscriptions. At Chartres the labyrinth consists of a geometrical figure in the form of a circle, with a diameter of about forty feet, in which the "labyrinthine ways" are arranged concentrically about a sixfoil centre-piece. The idea goes back to the legendary labyrinth of Daedalus in the palace of Minos in Crete, and commemorates him as the ancestor of all the celebrated architects of the Western world. The figure became, so to speak, his symbol. Whether the winding paths of the labyrinth on the floor of the church possessed any religious significance, as is sometimes supposed, we do not know. The former labyrinths of Reims and Amiens, which as

7—HG

at Chartres were inlaid in the nave floor, contained the
names of the master builders who worked on the cathedrals.
The labyrinth of Reims (Fig. 33) is known to have been a
geometrical figure shaped roughly square, its paths following
an angular course into an inner octagon through eight-sided
projecting bays at the four corners. In the panels at the
corners were recorded the names and symbols of the thirteenth-century "masters of the works". The symbols indicated
their calling as architects, and were apparently arranged in
the order of their periods of service. As no dates are given,
however, we are obliged to unravel their chronological

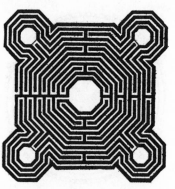

Fig. 33: REIMS, Labyrinth

sequence from other evidence.[1] The names run: Jean
d'Orbais, Jean de Loup, Gaucher de Reims, Bernard de
Soissons. The symbol and inscription of the middle panel had
already become illegible in the seventeenth century, but
probably recorded the name of Archbishop de Humbert,
who laid the foundation stone in 1211. From the octagonal
labyrinth of Amiens Cathedral, destroyed in 1825, the middle
stone has been preserved. Besides the name of Bishop Evrard
de Fouilloy, who laid the foundation stone in 1220, it also
gives the names of masters of the works active until 1288:

[1] Erwin Panofsky, *On the chronology of the four masters of Reims.* Jahrbuch
F. Kunstwissenschaft, 1925. Page 55 et seq.
    Walter Überwasser in *Kunstchronik*, 1949. Page 204.

Robert de Luzarches, Thomas de Cormont, and the latter's son, Renaud de Cormont. Possibly the middle stone of the labyrinth at Chartres bore the architects' names, but unfortunately no traces have survived.

The Sketchbook of Villard de Honnecourt

As their names show, the architects all came from the original district of Gothic. They were beyond question men of profound experience who, quite apart from the traditional bonds of the masons' lodges, were united to one another by the closest ties. From their buildings we can not only recognize their genius, but also appreciate the scholarship in architecture and the plastic arts, and the vast stores of wisdom and skill to be found on the building sites. Moreover, a single source has survived from which we can still obtain a clear insight into the nature of their work and of the practical, theoretical and artistic knowledge at their disposal. In the Bibliothèque Nationale in Paris (ms. fr. 19093) is preserved the sketchbook of Villard de Honnecourt, a master of the works from Picardy who was active about 1235, during the period when Chartres Cathedral was completed and those of Reims, Cambrai and Amiens were still under construction. His sketchbook, of which about half has come down to us, contains a mass of drawings, with explanatory notes on every aspect of the building crafts, technical procedure and artistic composition. It served as a text and model book for Gothic builders, and accompanied Villard on his journeys. The captions to the drawings and the descriptions are of course in thirteenth-century script and not easily intelligible to us without further explanation. The exemplary edition of the book by Hans R. Hahnloser,[1] however, embodies earlier researches and provides not only a detailed commentary, but elucidates the character and significance of the whole work.

The astonishing thing about this collection of details, which at first glance seems to have been compiled without method, is the impression which we finally gain from it that

[1] Hahnloser, *Villard de Honnecourt*. Vienna, 1935.

everything has its place in a grand all-embracing conception of art. Geometry is the guiding spirit and principle of the whole book, whether the author is concerned with the responsibilities of the master of the works, with maçonnerie, charpenterie or portraiture, with the calculation of proportions, with stone-cutting and the best building stones, with the measurement of angles and of the height of buildings, with the making of roof trusses, "engines" of all kinds, the construction of piers, towers and cloisters, or with drawings of figures according to proportions determined by geometry.

The spirit of geometry which characterizes the sketchbook is most noticeable when the fundamentals of building are under discussion. According to Villard de Honnecourt the halved, or bisected, square was the "true basis of art". "Here was an architecture without a yard-measure in which dimensions were still determined in the original way by setting out on the ground and by the relationship of basic architectural figures (like the square)."[1] From the application of simple structural geometry there emerged in Gothic, even for the elevations, the law "of the whole". Rule of thumb methods were used until the late middle ages. We must turn to Walter Überwasser's exposition of building "according to true measure" if we are to understand completely the reasoning which actuated Gothic architectural theories.

In Villard de Honnecourt's sketchbook, however, there is also vividly reflected the busy life of a master architect on the cathedral sites of the time. He may not have been one of the greatest, but he was trained scientifically in the thirteenth-century sense of the word, and had seen much of the world. As he himself states, he had been in many countries, his journeys taking him—on business—as far as Hungary, where he stayed some time. His drawings show that he knew the cathedrals of Laon, Chartres, Reims, Meaux and Cambrai, as well as the Cistercian church of Vaucelles and the cathedral of Lausanne. His part as a designer is revealed in the choir plan with double ambulatory and chevet chapels, which he devised, according to the text, in collaboration

---

[1] Walter Überwasser, *Nach rechtem mass*. Jahrbuch d. Preuss. Kunstsammlung. 1935. Page 264.

with Pierre de Corbie.[1] There was, therefore, consultation between architects, and it is significant that this took place over the Gothic architect's most difficult problem: the choir. The reproduction in the sketchbook of the ground plans of choirs in various churches which Villard knew is, therefore, to be expected. There are no nave plans, with the exception of a sketch plan of a Cistercian church. No reliable records

Fig. 34: VILLARD DE HONNECOURT

have survived to show what religious buildings he designed himself, but the Collegiate church of St. Quentin is a strong probability, its choir bearing a striking resemblance to that of Reims Cathedral. The studies for Reims Cathedral occupy a noteworthy place in the sketchbook because of their detail, and are important not only from the standpoint of architectural history—Villard drew plans which are not as executed—but also in showing us what features of a building appeared essential to the contemporary cathedral architect.

[1] Hahnloser. Plate 29.

With the elevation (one bay) of the nave interior and the corresponding exterior (Fig. 17), with the internal and external view of the chevet chapels and the elegant flying buttresses of the choir (Fig. 34), for which he saw the proposals on the site, the entire cathedral of Reims was revealed to him as an experienced architect in the form of drawings. In particular, he recorded on one special page the plan of the "piliers cantonnés" (compound piers) of the nave, of the piers separating the choir chapels and the projections of the side aisle bays, in addition to the most significant of the ribs and arches. Whatever is missing had probably been recorded on the lost pages of the sketchbook.

All these entries are important, not only because they enable us to obtain an insight into a cathedral architect's methods of study and work, but also in reflecting Villard's estimate of church buildings erected in his time, for he chose only what seemed to him the finest examples. This is clearly apparent from one of his comments. Before he went to Hungary, he drew the tracery window of Reims Cathedral, the most significant innovation in the vocabulary of cathedral form, and one which we also regard as important in the history of art. Here are his words:

"Ves ci une des formes de Rains des espases de le nef teles com eles sunt antre ii pilers. J'estoie mandes en le tierre de Hongrie, qant io le potrais por co l'amai io miex." "Here is one of the windows of Reims from a bay of the nave arranged between two pillars. I was commissioned to go to Hungary, when I drew it, because I liked it the best."

At Chartres he drew only the great rose window of the west front, making slight alterations, an apparent indication of the way in which tradition was interpreted on a Gothic building site, the original forms being retained and modified at the same time.

He also included a tower from the west façade of Laon (Fig. 35) and writes about it full of admiration: "I have been in many countries, as you can see from this book, [but] nowhere have I ever found a tower like the one at Laon" (Hahnloser). This is undoubtedly a judgment to which we should still subscribe today. In thirteenth-century German

architecture the towers of Bamberg and Naumburg cathedrals bear witness that Villard de Honnecourt was not alone
in his admiration. The sketchbooks of German architects
who visited the building sites of Northern France in the
thirteenth century certainly contained pages like Villard's.

This also held good for another field of Gothic cathedral

Fig. 35: LAON. Tower, according to VILLARD DE HONNECOURT

art. We not only find architectural models in Villard, but
examples selected, so to speak, for the sculptural requirements of cathedrals. It is clear that the master of the works
had to supervise the sculpture as well as the architecture, and
the work of the building craftsman. In Gothic, however,
architecture assumed unquestioned leadership, and all the
visual artists were subordinated to it. And so we see in
Villard's book, expressed in the artistic vocabulary of his
time—it was the classic period of French High Gothic—

representations of Christ, the Virgin Mary and the Apostles, scenes from the Passion, and allegorical figures, such as "Ecclesia", "Superbia" and "Humiltas". Then there are the animals, from lions to locusts, each of which had their particular significance in the cosmos of Christian symbolism and were all, like the entire cathedral, the product of the same intellectual principles. The lion is especially noteworthy (see illustration on cover), for Villard writes about it: "LEO Ves ci i lion si com on le voit p(ar) devant, (et) sacies bien q(u)'il fut contrefais al vif." "Leo. Here is a lion as seen from in front. Note carefully that it was drawn from life" (Hahnloser). It is obvious from this description that every age has its own form of "realism". In fact, of course, Villard drew his lion as mediaeval natural history knew and described it. The lioness was supposed to bring dead cubs into the world. On the third day the father wakened them to life by his roars. With Villard, however, its natural appearance was subordinated, like every other visual conception, to the laws of geometry. It was a Gothic lion!

The Gothic Idea of Space and the Buttress

But we are still confronted by the technical problems of cathedral building. At the time when the great masters of the thirteenth century, the men of genius, appeared, the purely technical difficulties had been largely solved, but this was not yet so with questions which arose from the classic system and from the task of finding a design, at once artistically pleasing and structurally sound. For the Early Gothic of Northern France the twelfth century can be regarded as the testing period in building technique. The basic task for the architect lay in how best to adjust the pressure of the vault on the nave walls to the increasing height of the interior. How, in other words, was it possible to erect such a wall, towering, weightless, parchment-thin, without the risk of its collapse from the effects of thrust and compression. From the interior the method by which the wonderful composition of soaring luminous space was achieved is not apparent. Romanesque masonry was so solid that the massive blocks of stone laid one upon another made the wall self-supporting. The Gothic solution consists in placing all the points of support for the wall on the outside, so that, in conformity with the division of the wall into load-bearing members and non-bearing panels, the thrust is taken only at certain fixed points (Fig. 19). For this purpose Gothic developed a technical system known as buttressing.

In the tribune gallery churches of French Early Gothic the galleries themselves acted as buttresses for the nave walls (Fig. 8). Those parts of the walls exposed to the pressure of the vault could be supported in this way by invisible buttressing, the masonry supports under the tribune roofs transferring the thrust to the buttress piers reinforcing the external walls of the side aisles. With the progressive heightening of the interior, however, the point of reinforcement tended to be too low, if it was to stay beneath the tribune roof. So it was now decided to make the reinforcement visible in the form of masonry supports or arches "flying" above the tribune roof. This was done from the last quarter of the twelfth century. Frequently these buttress arches were added after the completion of the building. The history of the flying buttress makes it clear that it was not until the idea of the Gothic interior had been realized that the technical problem of providing the cathedral with the necessary external support was tackled. Every alteration in the height of the interior and every modification in the cross-section presented the architect with fresh difficulties in finding the best solution for disposing the flying buttresses. At first their use was purely functional, but gradually they became part of the recognized language of architectural form with a decisive effect upon the external appearance of the cathedral.

A radical change in the basilical section of the cathedral occurred when the architect of Chartres dispensed with tribunes and had to reconsider the structural design of the buttressing, his task being accentuated by the much greater dimensions of the nave wall. Chartres Cathedral set a standard in this respect.

The architect treated the buttress system in a highly

original manner, giving the piers a towerlike form, from which powerful arches spring over the side aisles to engage the nave wall at two points (Figs. 3 and 36). The buttress piers also have a very distinctive pattern (Plate 6). The thickness of the masonry is first reduced in depth in two stages up to the level of the moulding which crowns the side aisles, these "steps" being emphasized on the external face by offsets.

The cornice of the side aisles is extended round the buttress piers. The upper parts of the piers, rising above the roofs of the aisles, are also stepped backwards towards the nave, whilst preserving their towerlike character. Noteworthy innovations were the narrow niches for sculpture in the external face of the buttress "towers". From these massive piers spring double arches to the nave wall and—a peculiar feature for a Gothic building—the two arches are linked by a composition resembling the spokes of a wheel. The latter consists of a very solidly constructed arcade of columns, splayed outwards to conform with the circular movement of the overall design. This produces a muscular, virile effect, which brings out clearly the powerful character of the abutments. The integration of the buttress system into the elevational design of the basilica compels admiration. The windows of the side aisles have the same breadth as the buttress piers. Unhappily the original appearance of the crown of the piers has been changed. A third flying buttress, which engaged the nave wall on the line of the guttering, was placed upon them in the fourteenth century to strengthen the clerestory—a purely functional device, which destroys the rhythmical design of the piers by concealing the chalice-shaped projection of the nave gallery with its bracket and support below. In the drawing from Viollet-le-Duc (I, p. 65) the original appearance is shown (Fig. 36).

In the choir of Chartres the wheel spoke motif is modified to the extent that the higher and lower flying buttresses are linked by a series of slim-pillared, pointed arches (the spandrels having circular openings). This later form, lighter and more elegant in comparison with the nave, has been rightly used by Grodecki to support his contention that the

Fig. 36: CHARTRES. Flying buttress (after VIOLLET-LE-DUC)

Fig. 37: REIMS Cathedral. Section

building of Chartres began with the nave and that the choir
followed somewhat later.[1]

As at Chartres, the buttress system of Reims Cathedral was
architecturally an important element in the appearance of
the exterior (Plate 29). In principle the conception of the

[1] L. Grodecki, "The Transept Portals of Chartres Cathedral." *Art Bulletin*,
1951. Page 156 et seq.

Fig. 38: REIMS Cathedral. Buttress piers

buttress support as a towerlike pier was retained at Reims, but by lightening the nave wall and, above all, by the invention of the tracery window, the architect was able to give the buttress system a new and exquisitely balanced form. The weight of the buttress piers, as at Chartres, is progressively reduced in a series of conspicuously defined steps (Figs. 37 and 38). At Reims the comparatively thin piers rise straight upwards and are, stage for stage, more delicately articulated, culminating in openwork tabernacles (surmounted by pointed turrets), in which angels stand with outstretched wings, so that the cathedral seems to be watched over from above by an angelic host. The two elegantly designed flying buttresses, which link the piers to the nave wall, are not joined to each other. The complete harmony with which the buttress piers are disposed in relation to the elevations of the nave is most impressive, as is the consistent extension of this design about the entire building, including the façades. For the choir, as in every cathedral where flying buttresses are used, the complicated ground plan produces a familiar structural and architectural problem, since the buttress system has to be disposed radially over double ambulatories. This was not the case with the nave of Notre-Dame in Paris, with its twin lateral aisles, because the nave wall above the inner aisle is supported by the tribunes. For Chartres and Reims the solution lay in doubling the buttress supports. An intermediate pier was introduced over the ambulatory. In Villard de Honnecourt's book an unexecuted proposal from the site workshops at Reims shows a very clear and effective arrangement (Fig. 34): slender, widely spaced piers, and two parallel flying buttresses engaging the nave wall through the intermediate pier, which is used as additional support. As Villard left out the flying buttresses in his drawing of the nave elevation in order to display the pattern of the wall clearly (Fig. 17), it is not apparent whether the scheme was to apply to the buttressing of the choir. The executed system of support differs considerably from Villard's drawing (cf. Hahnloser, Plates 78 and 79) and follows the form for the walls of the nave described above. The buttress system of Reims undoubtedly occupies a supreme place among the classic Gothic cathedrals.

At Amiens the great height of the interior demanded an elongated form for the buttress piers of the nave with a different type of substructure. In comparison with Reims, however, the piers seem austere, harsh, less ornamental, designed with mathematical precision exclusively for their

Fig. 39: Beauvais Cathedral. Choir

tectonic function (Fig. 18). This precision is especially
noticeable with regard to the chevet chapels, the buttress
system for the choir revealing in its style a later and more
elaborate conception in which, unlike the arrangement for
the nave, the twin flying buttresses are linked by a chain of
arches (Fig. 26).

The buttress systems for the choirs of the cathedrals of

Beauvais (Fig. 39) and Le Mans border on the fantastic, thanks to still further increases in height. The Gothic interior, in an endeavour to achieve the impression of an ethereal, unsubstantial weightlessness, was suspended, so to speak, upon a vast and highly ingenious structural framework.

7. THE EXTERIOR

THE EXTERIOR of the classic cathedral does not depend for its effect only upon the buttress system, which envelops the core of the building like a thick transparent shell, but upon a symmetrical grouping of masses, which is determined by the form of the façades and the disposition of the towers, both of them factors grounded in the tradition of Western sacred architecture. When one thinks that Chartres Cathedral, according to the layout of the ground plan (Fig. 14), was to have had three façades and nine towers (two for the west front, two above each transept portal, one over the crossing and one tower at either side of the apse), the unprecedented complexity of the architectural problems, which the architect of such a cathedral had to surmount in reaching his solution, is at once apparent. It meant that the special features of the building, the west, north and south fronts had to be brought into harmony with the nave elevations (Plate 4) and that the towers had to grow in an architecturally organic manner out of the main structure below them (Fig. 40). Only a genius could do this, but men of genius were to be found on the building sites of the classic cathedrals. At Reims the architect's brief was much the same, although the choir towers were left out. At Amiens, however, the idea of a multi-towered cathedral was modified (Plate 55). The crossing and transept towers were abandoned and the principal emphasis was placed upon a magnificent design for the west front.

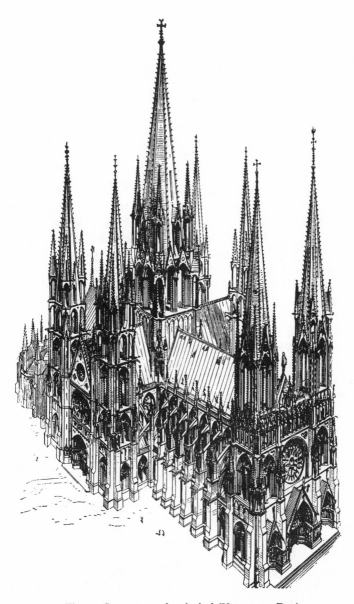

Fig. 40: Seven-towered cathedral (Viollet-le-Duc)

The Twin-towered Façade

A problem of architectural history now arises. How was the conception of the twin-towered façade, which evolved north of the Alps—in Italian mediaeval architecture, for example, façade and tower were always separated—introduced into the structural plan of the Gothic cathedral? In order to make plain the architectural problem which the designers of the great Gothic cathedrals had to solve, certain basic conditions, entailed in the erection of a twin-towered façade in association with a basilical nave, must be clarified. If we understand the "façade" to be an architectural expression of the basilical section of the interior, then the emphasis will lie on the middle, and the building will require the sides to be subordinated to the middle. Should two towers be incorporated in the façade, forming symmetrical flanking features, the tendency will be for the sides to be stressed at the expense of the middle (e.g., Cologne Cathedral). In the layout of the twin-towered façade, therefore, two mutually contradictory demands must be brought into harmony. To define the "façade" as the display front of the building, however, is an over-simplification, for it is a composition in depth, which reaches into the interior of the nave. The Gothic architect had to bear this in mind. Moreover, the façade structure contains the great portals, the main entrances. Their dimensions and axial relationship to the nave had equally to be taken into consideration. In actual fact the twin-towered façades of Early Gothic cathedrals display a dramatic advance and the greatest resource and variety in interpreting this majestic architectural problem.

The basic organization of a twin-towered façade was from the beginning invariable. It derived from the eleventh-century Norman fronts of the time of William the Conqueror and his wife, from St. Étienne, the church of the Abbaye-aux-Hommes, and from La Trinité, the church of the Abbaye-aux-Dames, both at Caen.

The massive substructure of St. Étienne (Fig. 41) comprises three sections, corresponding to the three aisles of the interior. These are separated by buttresses and adorned by

Fig. 41: Caen, Abbey church of St. Étienne (circa 1080)

round-arched windows, the middle section being wider than the other two. Horizontally, the main front is divided into entrance portal, gallery and clerestory. Vertically, it is noteworthy for the continuous buttresses, without ornament of any kind, rising almost to the full height of the façade and guiding the eyes to the open storey of the towers, which rise, on each side, from the massive self-contained block below, a wonderfully effective solution, reached with the simplest of means and satisfying equally the demands of both façade and towers.

The façade of La Trinité is differently conceived, the narrower lateral sections being handled in sharper contrast to the middle. The vertical treatment by means of buttresses is the same, although the flanking sections are more directly linked with the towers. The Gothic twin-towered façade also exploited the possibilities of a similar vocabulary of form, whilst continually altering the relationship of the various

Fig. 42: Senlis. West Front (circa 1180)

parts, introducing stylistic modifications to the structure and bringing fresh developments in interpreting the effect of the interior on the façade.

The façades of St. Denis (1137–1140) and Senlis (Fig. 42) owe their vitality to the restless contrast between the lateral sections and the broader middle piece. None of the storeys are even in height. At Senlis the façade consists of two slender towers with a rather elaborate composition between.

At Noyon the storeys are indeed of equal height, but the tower concept completely dominates the nave cross-section. The buttresses, with frequent offsets, extend to the base of the towers and are so massively constructed that they leave no space for developing the middle of the façade.

The celebrated façade of Notre-Dame in Paris (Fig. 43) shows for the first time an exquisitely proportioned design of the highest quality within the conditions imposed by the requirements of the building. It must also not be overlooked that the nave cross-section sets its own particular problem, for the façade had to serve as the front of a five-aisled, and not of a three-aisled, cathedral. Yet the façade is tripartite, while making due allowance in its breadth for the double aisles behind it. Each tower side rises above a double bay fronting two lateral aisles. The horizontal emphasis, frequently commented upon in stylistic appraisals of the façade, is a logical expression of the broad span of the interior. In the breadth of the tower sides there lay a risk that the middle would appear outweighted. The architect met this problem most happily by a rose window, which rises slightly higher than the crowns of the containing arches of the tower sides. Similarly, the central portal of the entrance floor rises appreciably above its neighbours. The vertical divisions, as always, are stressed by buttresses. These, however, do not follow an unbroken upward course, which might have over-emphasized the tower sides. If we take as a comparison the solid eleventh-century Norman front of Caen, it is clear that the openings in Paris, in the relationship between closed and open wall surfaces, determine the appearance of the façade, in which organic forms, recessed effects, lattice patterns and incised and moulded outlines all play their part. This is particularly Gothic. The exquisite balance between the parts and the whole—what we might describe as the mathematics of surface relationship—is particularly French. The delicate relief of the façade, the certainty with which the gallery of Kings (a novel feature) is extended in front of the buttresses, the open gallery above the rose storey which prepares for the unencumbered floor of the towers, the elegant precision with which the great portals are carved out of the façade, with

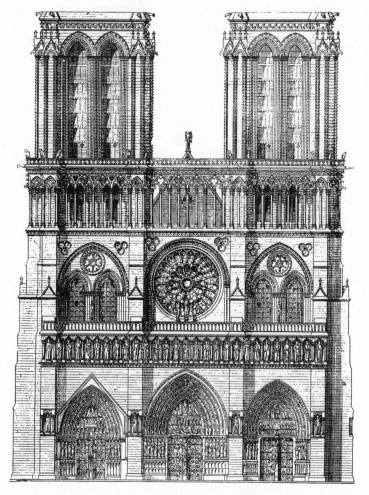

Fig. 43: PARIS, Notre-Dame. West Front (1200-1250)

which the curves are traced in the various openings of the rose storey and broken with gently pointed arches, and with which the intervals are calculated in the transparent, lace-like gallery above; all these are very Parisian.

The west front of Laon Cathedral (begun *circa* 1190, Fig. 44) contrasts most strongly with the architectural treatment

Fig. 44: LAON Cathedral. West Front (begun 1190)

of the west façade of Paris. With its three-aisled transepts, Laon was planned to have three twin-towered façades, and in this respect anticipated Chartres. The arrangement of the transept façades (*circa* 1180) reflects the elevations of the interior with splendid clarity, and enables the open tower storeys to rise from the substructure with apparent spontaneity. The west front is revealed as a dramatic, and strikingly vigorous, composition, characterized by the deeply recessed and salient features of the individual storeys, and in the middle by a rose set in a circular vaulted frame, surmounted by a daringly irregular gallery, behind which the open storey of the towers rises with wonderful freedom and structural logic. Georg Dehio said of this façade: "Whoever devised it was, if you like, a genius with traces of uncouthness, but a genius all the same, full of originality, felicity, gaiety and daring . . ." Villard de Honnecourt considered the towers the finest he had seen and copied them, noting the transition of the square substructure into octagonal turrets at the corners, a feature characteristic of Laon (Fig. 35). The octagonal corner projections of the transept towers were adorned with open tabernacles. We can also learn from Villard de Honnecourt how the unexecuted spires were intended to look.[1] They were to be open spires, the ribs decorated with crockets, the first time that this motif appeared in Gothic architecture. As only one tower was completed on each of the transept façades—their weight was too great—the many-towered effect of the original design cannot be fully appreciated. None the less this great church sited like a fortress on a hilltop, with the town clustered below it, is still one of the most compelling manifestations of French Early Gothic.

Chartres

We turn expectantly to the master of Chartres Cathedral to discover how precisely, after so much experience and brilliant experimentation on the building sites in and about Paris, he came to conceive the west front of his great building with

[1] At Notre-Dame in Paris, too, the spires were abandoned.

its novel cross-section designed without a tribune gallery. The peculiar history of the building of Chartres Cathedral, however, supplies us with the answer to this question (Fig. 45). The old building erected by Bishop Fulbert in 1020, which preceded the present cathedral, stood until 1194. In the twelfth century two massive towers were placed in front of the west end of Fulbert's church; the North Tower (1134–1150), which remained for the time being unfinished, and the South Tower, which was built from foot to finial in twenty-five years (1145–1170). Between the façade of the Fulbert building and the twelfth-century towers was a porch with a three-door portal aligned to the back of the towers, which were therefore originally exposed on three sides. For reasons which we do not know, the three-door portal, together with the group of three windows above, was brought forward into line with the west side of the towers. This was not achieved without a certain amount of forcing, of which evidence can still be detected in the way the flanking portal arches have been trimmed away at the sides. When the Fulbert building was destroyed by fire in June 1194—it was a three-aisled, flat-roofed building with an ambulatory, from which three chapels radiated, but without transepts— there survived, in addition to the great vaulted crypt which still extends underneath the nave and aisles, and the statue of the Virgin, the towers at the west end and the erections between them. In the new building, which was begun immediately, it was decided to incorporate these undamaged towers in the west front. The new master crowned the middle section with a rose window of consummate design, twenty-three feet in diameter, and adapted this composite structure, despite its lack of unity, into a twin-towered façade for his cathedral. But why did he leave the North Tower without a spire? Was it out of respect for the structural perfection of the South Tower (Fig. 45), completed a generation or two earlier? In fact it was not until the latest phase of Gothic that the North Tower was given a top (by Jean Texier at the beginning of the sixteenth century).

The master of the new cathedral must have started his building immediately after the fire. It remains an astonishing

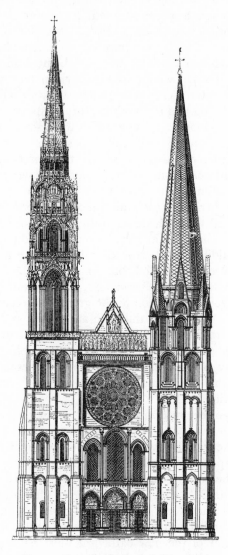

Fig. 45: CHARTRES Cathedral. West Front

fact that, while the old building was in flames, the bishop and chapter actually found the architect for this important task, and that he was able to submit at once a general plan, which developed radically new theories for the elevations and section, while making use of the still serviceable old foundations. Where did this architect of genius emerge from so quickly?

There is no doubt that the cathedral building sites were in close touch with one another and that the clients, the bishops and their chapters, knew where high talent was to be found. When in 1353 the Emperor Karl IV, in his palace at Prague, wanted to finish the cathedral, he summoned from Schwäbisch-Gmünd the young Peter Parler, who was only twenty-three years old! Admittedly the Parlers were a well-known German family of master-builders, but the confidence with which the imperial client entrusted this important commission to the young Parler—and his action was amply justified —is amazing.

We do not know whether the master of Chartres was a young, or already established, architect. I should like to believe that he was a product of the brilliantly resourceful team working on the cathedral site of Laon, for there are many points in common between the two buildings, and that it was from Laon that he took the decisive step forward which enabled him to create the new formal grammar of classic Gothic.

From this master, whose name we do not know, derives the basic plan of the many-towered cathedral of Chartres. But that does not mean that he himself saw the work through to the finish. The transept façades, designed to support twin-towers, but in the end built without spires, reveal in their final form so many new details of style that they suggest sources outside the master architect's vocabulary of forms.

According to the illuminating results of Louis Grodecki's researches (in the *Art Bulletin* for 1951), the form of the transept façades underwent in the course of time a transformation, which progressed from a simple composition (without a porch) in the manner of the transept façades of Laon, to more and more elaborate treatment, culminating in the erection of lavishly decorated porches in front of both the north and south portals. Here, however, we can dispense with the details of each individual phase of construction in order to obtain a general picture.

Both façades are very closely associated with the ground plan of the transepts (Figs. 14 and 46). The towers are placed over the side bays of the transepts without interrupting the orderly arrangement of the interior by massive free-standing piers. Both façades have a dominating effect on the inside of the church through their great rose and lancet windows. Externally the forms employed in composing these façades are already familiar to us from other Gothic structures of this kind, but at Chartres their application is distinguished by the particular manner in which the individual parts are dovetailed into one another and subordinated to the needs of the whole. In this we can see the classic character of the Gothic design of the façades at Chartres.

Because of breaks in continuity in the progress of the work, the north façade, although basically similar in structure, lacks the splendour which the south façade displays (Plate 4). The ultimate symmetry is lacking in details. The architect who erected the south façade in its final form achieved a perfect architectural solution. The rose, with the five lancet windows beneath, dominates the ensemble of each façade. The effect is enhanced by the small gallery over the rose and the upward prolongation of the two buttress piers which frame it. The way in which the open tower-storeys are subordinated to the middle section, whilst providing the necessary lateral support, and all wall surfaces, even the external face of the buttress piers, are covered with a system of colonnettes—a new method of taking the solidity and ungainliness out of heavy masonry—all this represents an incomparably subtle exercise in relationships, in which the basic theme of strict verticality, which also characterizes the sculpture of the portals, is hardly detectable.

It could be objected that this structural beauty is no more than the beauty of a truncated architectural body, the result of a failure to complete the twin-towered façade. In point of fact the spires were abandoned, just as the choir towers

Fig. 46: Chartres Cathedral. South Front

were extended to the roof line and then also left without spires. The architectural beauty of the transept façades could certainly have been preserved equally well if the master had set light constructions on the towers rather like the slender open storeys of Hugues Libergiers on the church of St. Nicaise at Reims (destroyed in the French revolution). But it appears that theories about the ideal appearance for a cathedral exterior had undergone some changes in the period around 1220. Many towers impaired the unity of the general effect. The twin-towered façade became at Chartres a "transept front", more appropriate to the grouping of the building as a whole than a composition with nine towers (Plate 4).

Amiens

From the first a uniform "enclosed" effect was sought for the massive structure of Amiens Cathedral, which was begun in 1220 (Plate 55). The ground plan is the same type as at Chartres and Reims; but, despite the three-aisled layout of the transepts, Robert de Luzarches, the designer, made provision for a twin-towered façade at the west end only. The transept arms are faced with a tall middle section set between stepped, and steeply rising, buttresses. Over this are traced two principal stringcourses which correspond exactly to those embracing the walls of the aisles and nave. The heights at which these mouldings are placed are also identical with those defining the stages of the west front. But it is clear that this sumptuous west façade (Fig. 47), with its cavernous portal entrances between prominent buttress piers, with its galleries and tower openings—the familiar vocabulary in fact used by the other classic cathedrals— lacks any reliable sense of proportion in relating the various parts to one another, even if we make allowance for the open storey above the rose being a later addition. The façade has often been criticized on architectural grounds. To place the two galleries directly on top of one another was as unfortunate as the way in which the rose was squeezed out of the middle and forced beneath the cornice at the top of the façade.

Fig. 47: AMIENS Cathedral. West Front

Reims

In Reims Cathedral (begun in 1211) on the other hand, the external elevations of the transepts were conceived at first with twin-towered façades, but were not carried out, as they were at Chartres, as "show fronts" with portals and porches. (The two portals on the north side were only added in the course of time as a result of changes to the plan.) In its design as a many-towered cathedral (Fig. 40), the exterior as a whole recalls Laon and Chartres. But at Reims, as well, the construction of the transept towers was abandoned in favour of the west façade because of altered notions about the nature of the perfect building. As the transepts at Reims are one bay shorter than those of Chartres they do not jut out so far. The harmony with the elevational system of the nave and with the architecture of the buttresses seems complete. In particular, the continuation of the lines of the stringcourses round the transept façades contributes decisively to this impression. The middle is dominated by the tracery rose window, floating under a pointed arch. Beneath it, and corresponding to the triforium (inside), is a series of three arches, each framing a small circular window with a sexfoil panel. The tower sides are pierced, next to the rose, by coupled tracery windows. The buttress piers are decorated with tabernacles and pinnacles like those of the nave.

In Reims we have the answer to the question "How did a classic cathedral construct its west front in the golden age of Gothic?" (Fig. 48). The actual time of building lasted well beyond the thirteenth century, although the High Gothic conception was preserved. The west façade of Reims combines all the architectural experience acquired from earlier realizations and, in its basic arrangement, apparently tried out in the transept fronts, but enriched by the architectural knowledge exemplified in the façades of Laon, Paris and Chartres. In addition, the elevation of the west front at Reims reflects the articulation of the nave, both inside and out. None of the great Gothic cathedrals of this type pays so much respect to uniformity in the general impression of the whole design as does Reims. One hardly notices that the

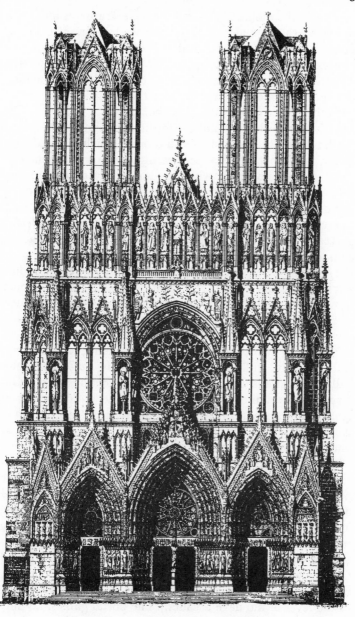

Fig. 48: REIMS Cathedral. West Front

heights of the mouldings round the nave, transepts and choir are not exactly maintained on the west front. The string-course under the rose is placed lower than the corresponding one extending along the nave, out of consideration for the architectural form of the tower storey, while the moulding above it is somewhat higher than the cornice surmounting the other external elevations of the church.

This façade displays an extraordinary richness of contrast within a rigidly imposed overall design, which is based on a single fundamental idea permeating every constituent element. We do not know which to admire most: the capacity of the master to perfect every detail of form without losing sight of the effect of the whole; or his ability to dispose, with unerring certainty, the wealth of features of a vastly differing succession of storeys, so that they achieve a balanced relationship with the middle axis. When we say that every form on the façade is a perpendicular, this is certainly true, but it does not indicate very much. What matters at Reims is the manner in which it is done. Everything has become sharper, slimmer, steeper, more elegant. As at Laon and Chartres, verticality gives a decidedly imposing effect to the façade. If we compare the fronts of Paris, Laon, Chartres and Reims, which do not differ to any wide extent chronologically and geographically, the astonishing resourcefulness in the formal vocabulary of the architecture developed on the building sites of Northern France, raising to the highest artistic level so many variations on the theme of the twin-towered façade, is at once apparent. One can certainly see how much the façade of Reims Cathedral owes to Laon, and yet everything at Reims is new. The novelty begins at ground level with the portals. With their deep porchlike bays, their rich sculptural ornamentation covering the face of even the buttress piers, and their stepped gables, they constitute a kind of triumphal order. (A curious feature occurs in the composition of the portal, the tympana of the arches consisting of tracery windows opening into the interior, while in one, unique, instance the motif of the great rose is brought down to the level of the nave arcades.) The portal gables, lavishly enriched with sculpture, their outlines softened by crockets, rise into the storey above, breaking the horizontal silhouette of the triforium stage.

On the rose storey, where there is a much looser relationship of all parts between the pinnacled buttress-piers, the contrast is expressed between the narrow tower openings with their lattice tracery and the wide middle piece, somewhat in the manner of Chartres, although Reims dramatizes this alternation of features. The rose, like a great wheel in the middle, is slung between an open pointed arch, a device already employed on the transept fronts; the west rose, however, exhibits a finer, more delicate and more elaborate design. Above the rose storey is set the gallery of Kings, which binds together once again the three vertical parts of the façade in an even, close-packed rank, before giving way to the open storey of the towers. Without impairing the balance of the whole, the towers are most happily anticipated in the tower sides of the rose storey. In the adornment of the flanking octagons with open turrets we meet once more a feature of Laon, but at Reims everything is handled in a more disciplined, incisive and uniform manner. In addition, the dominating vertical tendency is everywhere held discreetly in check, so that it does not become exaggerated or develop into an exercise in exclusively vertical forms. The horizontal lines in the organization of the façade of Reims suitably counterbalance the assertive upward emphasis of the design as a whole. In this sense of proportion, in the unfailing perception, apparent in every subtle refinement of form, in the appropriate placing of each element in the architectural composition, lies the quality which we recognize as "classic".

Paul Valéry once referred to the happy combination of fantasy and logic as one of the specific characteristics of the European spirit. It is this characteristic which inspires and adorns a creation like the west front of Reims Cathedral.

8. PORTALS AND SCULPTURE

The Story of Mankind's Salvation

WE CANNOT fully comprehend a Gothic cathedral without taking into consideration the imagery in the form of sculpture and stained glass, which constitutes an important ingredient of the architecture. With the sculpture, the object was not so much to enrich the architectural effect by decoration, although this requirement was also fulfilled, but to bear visible witness to the canons of Christian belief and to reflect the intellectual climate in which mediaeval men felt at home. The scope was nothing less than a general history of mankind with Our Lord as the central figure, man's beginning and end as the twin poles of the story of his salvation, and a panoramic exposition of the entire religious life of the thirteenth century.

Not every Gothic cathedral succeeded in this dedicated task. But the three great classic cathedrals of France seem to have had inexhaustible resources in pictorial narrative. Chartres Cathedral alone has some 1,800 works of sculpture, and it is much the same at Reims and Amiens, so that we are offered a most remarkable view of the metaphysical fabric of the thirteenth century and of its attitude towards art, even when we confine ourselves exclusively to these three cathedrals.

This iconographical pageantry is subordinated to a strict and most carefully considered plan, both in subject matter and artistic treatment, which is not readily intelligible without some appreciation of its mediaeval genesis. Gothic, like all Christian art, uses the human figure to embody certain definite ideas, but develops in the process a language of its own and finds opportunities, in comparison with the early mediaeval period, of giving tangible expression to new factors. Gothic sculpture was closely and fundamentally related to architecture. It could not have existed without it, and had no place as an independent art, as it did in the classical age, or does today. The starting point for this alliance between sculpture and architecture was the portal, as indeed it had been in Romanesque days. Thus, in the classic cathedrals the entrance to the holy places is also an introduction to the world of religious symbolism and pageantry.

Types of Portal

The sculptures are grouped according to the specific themes which they portray and are so fitted into the portal architecture that the whole of each portal is devoted to one subject. The tympanum, as the middle feature, initiates the theme, while the surrounding voussoirs and jamb columns illustrate related ideas and episodes. The iconography of the carved figures in Gothic portal architecture reflects certain cycles of events. Definite types of portal emerge, and within the framework of their particular themes a wide variety of artistic interpretation was possible. These types are:

1. *Last Judgment Portal*, which depicts the whole sequence of events at the end of the world. Portals of this type form the middle doorway to the south transept of Chartres (Plate 23), and provide access to the north transept of Reims (Plate 33) and, in the centre bay, to the west front of Amiens (Plate 56).

2. *Virgin Portal*. The creation of portals in which the sculpture is devoted to the Mother of God was a particular feature at the end of the twelfth century, when the cult of the Virgin assumed a place of great importance. All three classic cathedrals of French Gothic are dedicated to Mary and honour her as their patroness. Thus at Chartres, where homage to Blessed Mary was a tradition dating far back into the early middle ages, the theme of the Virgin forms the centre piece of the north transept entrance (Plate 15). At Amiens we find it in a flanking portal of the west front and at Reims at the centre of the three great doors (Plate 42).

3. *Saints' (or Martyrs') Portal*. Veneration of the Saints was characteristic of the whole middle ages in every country, to an extent, indeed, that we can only with difficulty imagine

nowadays. Life in its entirety and in all its complexities was passed in the company of the Saints. "When a Christian had to endure heavy trials, when his mind was troubled and his soul was sad, he could always call to mind the name of some doughty saint to bring him comfort" (Mâle). Whoever wishes to obtain a clear view of the way in which the Saints were regarded in the High Gothic period and in which their Christian virtues were extolled, whoever wants to know about their lives and their deeds, should turn to the *Legenda Aurea* of Jacobus de Voragine. Jacobus, who took his name of Voragine from a place near Genoa, belonged to the Dominican order and between 1263 to 1273 recorded in picturesque Latin every story connected with the lives of the Saints and set them down according to the Calendar of the Church's year. One of the most remarkable and instructive books of legends of the time, often translated into the vernacular tongues and in constant use, this work is imbued with the same spirit which we find in the contemporary visual arts.[1] We shall meet these tales most frequently in the splendid stained glass of Chartres Cathedral, and in the Saints whom we find on the portals, each one significant in his capacity as patron of some church in the surrounding district (Plate 50).

The Portail Royal of Chartres

These "classifiable" portal types acquired their particular artistic character in the great cathedrals after the rebuilding of Chartres in 1194. The highly complicated and often obscure early history of the origins of Gothic portal architecture and iconography in the twelfth century cannot be discussed here. But, from among its various manifestations, there is one example which we cannot overlook, for it is at Chartres. This is the portal between the two towers of the west façade, celebrated as the "Portail Royal", which dates from about fifty years before the building of the new cathe-

[1] Jacobus de Voragine. *Legenda Aurea.* German translation by Richard Benz. Jena, 1917 (Vol. I); 1921 (Vol. II). New edition in one volume. Lambert Schneider, Verlag, 1955–1956.

PORTALS AND SCULPTURE 121

dral, but occupies none the less a prominent place in the art history of the second half of the twelfth century (Plate 11). As an expression of Early Gothic art it commands the deepest admiration. An extremely thorough examination of this portal, by Wilhelm Vöge, was published in 1894 under the title *Die Anfänge des monumentalen Stils im Mittelalter. Eine Untersuchung über die erste Blütezeit französischer Plastik.*

The Portail Royal does not belong to any of the types described above. It is a portal with three doorways, the tympanum of the middle one showing Christ in Majesty surrounded by the four Apocalyptic beasts (the Evangelistic symbols). Of the side portals, the right-hand (south) bay is devoted to the Incarnation, with the Majesty of the Virgin depicted on the tympanum; the tympanum of the north portal illustrates the Ascension. The lintels and voussoirs are also embellished with sculpture. The capitals carry small figures, representing from left to right, in the manner of a frieze, scenes from Our Lord's life, while the columns at the sides, in Vöge's view, depict "the ancestors of Christ" or, according to Mâle, patriarchs and prophets. The whole composition is in theme a "Christ Portal" with Our Lord as the dominant in the middle.

Certain fundamental characteristics of Gothic portal structure and figure design should be noticed here. The Gothic portal is set back, that is to say, it narrows from front to back, through the thickness of the wall and towards the doorway, in a succession of steps. The lintel is placed over the doorway on the jambs and above it lies the tympanum, which is framed by the voussoirs. In the setbacks of the side walls are columns, to which large carved figures are fixed, so that we speak of "column figures". This does not imply that these figures perform the function of columns like the caryatids of Antiquity. The Gothic column figure is a creation of a peculiar kind. Just as Gothic architecture, in the form of its artistic expression, pays little attention to the laws of gravity —and in this respect it is in complete conflict with the ideas of Antiquity—so the Gothic carved figure can hardly be considered "earthbound". It differs significantly from the characteristic statuary art of the Antique figure, for which "to stand" implies "to hold upright", material weight being overcome by the manner in which the load is supported. Thus the statuary problem of classical Antiquity depended upon the distribution, movement and support of the physical object. The statue is a "body" moulded to man's deliberate intention, held harmoniously erect by its own weight.

The Gothic figure is nothing of the kind. It is designed to give an impression of weightlessness, although its solidity is clear enough (Plate 13). It avoids any appearance of standing firm in the way that the figure is not set on the "ground" or on a socle (to represent it), but seems essentially detached from the ground, indeed the function of standing as a physical action is largely hidden. This concealment is made possible because it is a wall figure. In the classical age the wall served to set off the statue. In Gothic the wall itself is part of the composition. The Gothic figure has no existence in itself; it needs architecture in order to fulfil its purpose, and it fulfilled its purpose as a "column figure", as we see it at Chartres in the Portail Royal. Chartres does not offer the only column-figure portal of the period, but the most distinguished. The Chartres figures do not stand, but are detached from the ground with feet pointing down and away from the columns, and suspended in space in a kind of hovering attitude. The effect is enhanced by the way in which they contrast with the richly patterned background in the recessed angles of the wall, facing strictly to the front, unconcerned with their neighbours, looking like enchanted beings from another world.

It is abundantly apparent that the group of three portals of the Portail Royal was planned as a single composition. On close inspection, however, considerable differences are revealed in the overall design, differences of style in the sculpture and of skill in execution, which were acutely analysed by W. Vöge in 1894. We can accordingly distinguish various sculptors, who worked under a master in charge, and obtain some idea of the nature of their joint endeavours, although we shall not follow these in detail here. It will be enough to say that one chief master, four subordinate masters and several assistants can clearly be recognized from their work, and among the assistants were highly accomplished craftsmen.

To the chief master we owe the tympanum of the middle portal, together with the lintel and the large wall figures of the same portal, and those on the inner sides of the flanking portals. The tympanum represents the *majestas domini*: Christ in His glory (with the mandorla), surrounded by the Evangelistic symbols, an illustration of the transcendent supremacy of Christ, as it was always regarded in the early middle ages (Plate 12). Mediaeval art established a vocabulary of form for the symbolic representation of the divine world. The presiding master of the Portail Royal of Chartres brought to his interpretation a sublime power and dignity of expression. The composition is disposed in the tympanum in an admirably balanced and harmonious manner. The beasts are not of equal size, and the varied character of their relationship to the middle feature is extremely impressive. According to the translation, they are described as "beasts" in the Vision of St. John, but they are supernatural beasts, creatures of fantasy. The text (Revelation, iv. 7) says: "And the first beast was like a lion, and the second beast like a calf, and the third beast had a face as a man, and the fourth beast was like a flying eagle." Their use as symbols of the four Evangelists dates from early Christian times. On the tympanum at Chartres the winged apocalyptic beasts are treated not so much like heraldic devices, but as a kind of spiritual conception, participating dramatically in the divine revelation and with expressions of the utmost solemnity.

On the lintel under the tympanum are seated the twelve Apostles in groups of three. At either end of the row are single standing figures, which have not been identified with certainty. In the innermost row of the voussoirs appear twelve angels and in the two outer ones are the twenty-four elders of the Apocalypse with musical instruments.

In the side portal to the right (south), which is dedicated to the Incarnation, we see on the two rows of the lintel, under the enthroned Virgin, episodes from Mary's life, with the Annunciation, the Visitation, the Nativity, the Adoration of the Shepherds and the Presentation in the Temple.

The composition is so arranged that the infant Jesus is exactly on the middle axis.

Surrounding the Virgin, on the voussoirs, we find figures representing the Seven Liberal Arts, in which the sum of secular knowledge was represented to the middle ages (Plate 14). The distinctions between the Trivium (Grammar, Rhetoric and Dialectic) and the Quadrivium (Arithmetic, Geometry, Astronomy and Music) were rooted in Antiquity, and became symbolized in the literature of the early middle ages by persons. These were subsequently adopted in plastic art. There is nothing remarkable about their entry into the field of monumental sculpture in the Portail Royal, for there was a celebrated school at Chartres. The arts themselves are represented by female figures identifiable by their attributes. Thus Grammar holds a birch, Astronomy a measuring instrument, Music is striking bells with a hammer, and so on. In the Portail Royal each of the Seven Liberal Arts is associated with a man of learning from classical Antiquity. Although they are not designated by name, we know from our knowledge of mediaeval theory that eminent authorities like Donatus, Cicero, Aristotle, Euclid, Ptolemy and Pythagoras were in mind. In the lowest sections of the voussoirs of the Virgin Portal we find most expressive representations of thinkers and philosophers at their desks, engaged in their intellectual disputations.

Not only are the philosophical activities of mankind woven into the pattern of ideas for the Portail Royal at Chartres, but even the passage of time is depicted by symbolic figures and devices. On the voussoirs of the left-hand portal, which illustrates on the tympanum the Ascension of Christ with the Apostles watching from the lintel below, are representations of the months and the signs of the Zodiac. The months are indicated by the appropriate labours of man. For the middle ages this meant the peasant, the producer of food, sowing, reaping and hunting. The signs of the Zodiac are coupled to them by figures well known from the days of Antiquity.

The artistic power which dominates and permeates the whole composition is nowhere more eloquently expressed than in the large column figures which, according to Vöge, represent the genealogy of Christ; or, in Mâle's view, Biblical characters from the Old Testament.[1] They have an air of belonging to another world. Their high artistic standard is revealed in every detail with which the master of genius invested these strongly defined, cylindrical, attenuated forms and in the delicate lines of the drapery (Plate 13). They confront us with a touching candour and self-assurance in the uncompromising idiom of Early Gothic, heralding a new era of monumental figure sculpture, in which the novelty lies in the evident humanity of expression. In their faces shines the magic of personality, and it is this momentous new quality which marks the birth of Gothic sculpture in Europe.

Virgin Portals

When we turn from the Portail Royal at Chartres to the north transept façade, we enter quite another world (Plate 15). Roughly half a century divides the former from the initiation of the scheme for the north front, and in the meantime the tasks for the sculptors had multiplied. The original idea at Chartres was to confine the sculptural ornamentation to the portals, but a plan for the addition of porches was soon conceived, so that on the north side (as well as later to the south) there are three portals, corresponding to the three-aisled layout of the transepts, with a range of gabled porches. In addition, the dimensions of the portals were increased, and an elaborate pattern of sculpture was spread over them. The entire Biblical world seems to unfold before us. From the story of the Creation on the outer voussoirs of the central porch we progress by way of countless episodes and characters from the Old Testament to the Incarnation of the Saviour and the glorification of his Mother. The method of treatment changes and the vocabulary of forms changes also. How could it possibly be otherwise with such a prodigious abundance of sculpture? The practised eye can distinguish several masters, many hands and a marked

[1] Mâle, *L'art religieux du XIIe siècle en France*. 3rd edition, 1928. Page 392.

individuality among the artists.[1] But the amazing thing is not the many voices of the choir, but the skill with which they are subordinated to the needs of the whole. We can imagine the baton of an invisible conductor allotting with flawless precision to every man his proper part.

The portal architecture itself advanced along the lines on which it had started in Early Gothic. The column-figure portal with the fundamental qualities which we have already seen in the Portail Royal was the field in which developments took place. The unbroken continuity and unerring logic of the evolution of a dominant artistic idea, and the brilliant emergence of entirely new and startling formal possibilities out of existing resources are among the most wonderful features of the growth of French Gothic sculpture.

In the middle of the façade stands the Virgin Portal. This theme had emerged in the last decades of the twelfth century as a distinct type, represented in the Virgin portals of Senlis and Laon and now adopted by Chartres. The associations with Laon appear particularly close, as the brilliant researches of W. Sauerländer have shown in many instances.[2]

In the Gothic period the artist's field of inspiration for interpreting veneration for the Virgin was not confined to what we know about her from the Gospels, but included popular legends, from which particular scenes were chosen. The climax of adoration is reached in the coronation of Mary as Queen of Heaven (Plate 16) by her divine Son. Below, and preceding it in theme, is the Death of Mary, with the Apostles, "her beloved sons and brothers", gathered at her wish about her bed, while Christ receives her soul into heaven (the Assumption). Next to this, we see Mary's body being carried away by angels. These three scenes form a group on the tympanum of the portal. Around them, on the voussoirs, is a garland of angels with the precursors of

[1] Wilhelm Vöge, *Die Bahnbrecher des Naturstudiums um 1200.* Ztschr. f. bildende Künste, 1913–1914. Page 193 et seq.
   Kurt Bauch, *Chartres und Strassburg.* Oberrheinische Kunst; IV, 1929–1930. Berichte. Pages 33–35.
   Gottfried Schlag, *Die Sculpturen des Querhauses der Kathedrale von Chartres.* Wallraf-Richartz-Jahrbuch, 1943. Page 115 et seq.
[2] Willibald Sauerländer, *Beiträge zur Geschichte der frühgotischen skulpturen.* Ztschr. f. Kunstgeschichte, 1956. Page 1 et seq.

Christ (the Tree of Jesse) depicted individually. On either side of the portal openings appear prophets and patriarchs and, in particular, those whose prophecies and utterances, according to mediaeval interpretation, refer to Christ (Plate 17). At Chartres there are five to each side (four on the portal walls), but we should not know their names or realize their significance if it were not for their attributes. It must be understood, however, that the middle ages considered certain events, actions and characters in the Old Testament portended what was to come to pass in the New. By the entrance stands David, the prototype of Christ with the crown of thorns and spear. Next come Samuel with the sacrificial lamb and knife, Moses with the Tables of the Law and the brazen serpent, Abraham with Isaac in fetters (a reference to the sacrifice of Christ), and Melchisedek as king and priest, holding a chalice and censer in his hands. Opposite stand Isaiah with the flowering rod and a scroll (he had foretold the birth of the Virgin from the line of Jesse), Jeremiah with the halo and cross, Simeon with the infant Jesus in his arms, John the Baptist with the sacrificial lamb and, finally, St. Peter, recognizable by the great key, forming a link with the New Testament. At the feet of all these statues are small symbolic figures, related in significance to the larger figures above them. There is one other point of particular interest: on the trumeau of the doorway of a Virgin Portal, beneath the tympanum, one would expect the Mother and Child, as in Paris, and at Laon, Amiens and Reims. At Chartres we find instead Mary's mother, St. Anne, with Mary in her arms (Plate 63).

In comparison with Early Gothic examples, the Virgin Portal of Chartres reveals a new sense of form and a balanced relationship between the individual parts and the whole. The composition is better constructed. There is a new feeling of scale. For the first time the group under the baldachino depicting Mary's Coronation receives the place of honour. The scenes on the lintel of her death and Ascension are deliberately subordinated to the Crowning (Plate 16), which was not the case at Laon or in Paris. In addition, the design of the jambs impresses by the clarity with which the parts are disposed to contrast with one another within a unified whole, the figures with the ringed shafts of the socles, the salient with the recessed, the patterned with the plain, the ranks with the single files.

The Gothic column figure had evolved considerably in the course of a few decades from the rigid stylization which we see in the Portail Royal of Chartres. It is no longer strictly frontal and some attention is now given to movement, especially in the pose of the head. Nor is each figure treated as a separate conception, but a kind of mutual association becomes perceptible, expressed in the handling of the draperies of the closely packed figures. The possibilities of rhythmically grouped compositions now appear. Moreover, these statues of the Virgin Portal, especially the slim, attenuated figures on the David side, are handled with a certain delicacy of line, and this delicacy determines also the expression of the heads, which are not shaped like those of the Portail Royal at Chartres according to individual and personal characteristics. But these Virgin Portal figures also live on that super-terrestrial plane where there is no solid ground beneath their feet and where they are free of earthly limitations, a brotherhood present in body, but born of the spirit, identifiable as saints by their aureoles, poised under baldacchini, which like architectural crowns bestow on each his own particular dignity.

The World Centred in Christ

In order to appreciate the wealth of ideas deriving from mediaeval theology which received a collective, tangible interpretation in this form, we must not merely be able to "see" them, but to "read" them as well, both as isolated figures and in their context and mutual relationships. We shall then realize that portals of this kind are records in monumental sculpture of the history of the world. If we take the side portals and later the south façade of Chartres which illustrates the ideas of the New Testament, we shall gain some insight from these hosts of figures into that exclusive world with Christ as its centre visualized by the middle ages, a world cosmically ordered, artistically organized and conditioned by the same grandeur in its conception of form as the architecture which it inspired.

The pattern of ideas dominating the iconography of the Virgin Portal of the north transept of Chartres is continued in the side portals. On the jambs to the left are figures representing the Annunciation and the Visitation (Plate 18), accompanied by prophets. On the tympanum and lintel are the Nativity, the Adoration of the Shepherds and the Adoration of the Magi. On the voussoirs we first see angels with candles, then the parable of the Wise and Foolish Virgins, the conflict of the Virtues and Vices, and finally a dance of twelve queens, the twelve fruits of the Holy Ghost, with which Mary was endowed.

The right-hand (west) portal is entirely devoted to events and characters of the Old Testament, foreshadowing, according to the interpretation of the middle ages, the life and sufferings of the Saviour. On the tympanum is depicted the story of Job. His torment and humiliation—the sufferer lies on a pile of dung, surrounded by his wife and friends—alludes to Christ's Passion. The lintel shows the Judgment of Solomon. On the voussoirs we can study scenes from the lives of Samson and Gideon, the stories of Esther and Judith (Plate 21) and of Tobias and Tobit. Samson, carrying away the gates of Gaza, is the symbol of Our Lord's Resurrection. "Tobias, who restores his aged father's sight, is Jesus Christ bringing the light of God to an erring people" (Mâle). The large jamb figures of this portal are Jesus the Son of Sirach, Judith and Joseph (who, like Jesus Christ, was betrayed by his friends); and, on the other side, Balaam, the Queen of Sheba and Solomon (Plate 19). Solomon symbolizes Christ. The Queen of Sheba, with a negro slave at her feet, represents the heathen world and also, in her close relationship to Solomon, the Church (Ecclesia).

The narrative style of the Solomon Portal is startlingly vivid, and in this respect it differs from the other two. W. Vöge was the first to draw attention to the sculptor's individuality as an artist, calling him the "master of royal heads", and comparing his realism to Donatello.

The Expression of the Soul

The twelve scenes on the voussoirs from the story of Tobias and Tobit are wonderful indeed. Tobit is among the most colourful, enthralling, fantastic books of the Bible. The Gothic sculptor of the Solomon Portal evidently understood this, without laying much stress upon the meaning of its symbolism. This is apparent from the coherent handling of the whole design. Within the limits of his theme and medium the sculptor's virtuosity is astonishing (Plate 20). All the rich variety of human emotions is expressed, the changes of mood, the cares and doubts, the hopes and apprehensions. Even the journey of the young Tobias, accompanied by the angel Raphael and the dog, and the scene where Tobias catches the fish, are represented in this group of sculptures. Subjects like these were eagerly sought and depicted by artists right up to the Baroque period, but by painters, who included Rembrandt, rather than sculptors. Rembrandt constantly returned to the story of Tobit in order to illustrate the human and the miraculous, strife and harmony, piety and divine protection in workaday settings. The scene in which the blind Tobit suspects his wife of stealing the kid occurs (in 1626) among Rembrandt's early works, and again in a picture of 1646, but it had already appeared on the Solomon Portal of Chartres. This is not merely a problem of iconography, but has to be understood in relation to the development of Western art. It must not be forgotten that Gothic discovered and brought to light the whole emotional range of the human soul. This distinguishes it from the art of the early middle ages. In Gothic even the Creator is shown to have human feelings. When we look at the story of the Creation, God the Father is not shown in monumental sculpture. He is represented as Christ with the cross and halo. On the voussoirs (illustrating the story of the Creation) He appears as a full participant, anxious, contemplative, reflective. It is His face which chiefly expresses these emotions—a first indication of emphasis upon the human side of the Christ figure.

With discoveries such as these Gothic prepared the ground

for the expressive possibilities developed in art during the centuries which followed. The Renaissance regarded the world as compounded of tangible realities, individually calculable, spatially ordered. Nevertheless, the post-mediaeval period, both south and north of the Alps, was still dominated by Gothic, and the story of Tobit at Chartres makes it abundantly obvious that the profound imaginative painting of a Rembrandt had Gothic roots.

But the master of the Solomon Portal, all the same, was a man before his time. It was only in cathedral ground that seeds like his could germinate. They still had no place in the ordinary affairs of man, in his joys and sorrows and passions, but were confined to his relationship with God, for the cathedral was intended to present the history of the world as the history of salvation through Christ. The crucial factor about his prematurity, despite its signs of emancipation, is not that it foreshadowed wider possibilities to come, but that the master adapted his progressive views to the repertoire of ideas and architecture of the portal fabric.

The cycle of themes centred in the Virgin was never exploited with such variety as in the north portal of Chartres. Gothic architects undoubtedly had a theological programme before them, but this became modified in the process of artistic interpretation, so that now these, now those, features assumed sharper prominence. To this the effects of changes on the building site might contribute, reflecting differing stylistic standards in the craftsmen's lodges. As W. Vöge has pointed out,[1] "... the initiative of the master was often more important than the wishes of the client".

The Classic High Gothic Portals of Amiens

At Amiens the subject of Mary is not interpreted in a different sense, but in quite a different form, from that of Chartres. The whole artistic aspect of the Virgin Portal at Amiens, however, cannot be appreciated without regard for the entire tripartite composition of the portal as the under part of the west façade. The subordination of each individual

---

[1] W. Vöge, *Die Bahnbrecher* . . . Ztschr. f. bildende Kunst, 1913–1914.

component to the unit of form immediately above it is the
dominating principle here.

   Amiens Cathedral was begun in 1220 by Robert de
Luzarches and, so far as the principal parts of the façade are
concerned, finished in one uninterrupted operation by 1236.
The portal group also belongs to this period (Plate 56). The
uniformity of the design, the bold lines of the architecture,
the disciplined style of the monumental sculpture, combined
with the grandeur of the formal conception, which owes
more to the architect than the sculptor, justify us in speaking
of this portal as typical High Gothic, but in another sense
from that of the transept façades of Chartres and quite apart
from major differences in artistic interpretation. In the
general effect it matters a great deal whether the original
plan was gradually modified on the site (as happened with
the porches at Chartres) or whether the whole scheme was,
so to speak, poured out of a single mould, as at Amiens.
"Lift up your heads, O ye gates, and be ye lift up, ye ever-
lasting doors: and the King of glory shall come in." This,
surely, is the impression created by the work of the master-
designer, Robert de Luzarches.

   The three towering portals with the dominating centre-
piece of the Last Judgment combine in presenting a superb
architectural composition; to a certain extent portal and
porches are amalgamated. The deep extension of the portal
bays is emphasized by the way in which the master incorporated in his scheme the powerfully projecting buttress piers,
across the base of which the portal structure is evenly distributed. The gables, adorned with crockets, are thrust
similarly forward, so that the portals stand flush with the
buttress piers.

   In designing the elevation the architect had to take into
consideration the marked increase in height of the portal
storey, corresponding to the increased height of the lateral
aisles. He therefore inserted a double socle of an entirely
new and original kind. Over a delicate, but plainly patterned, substructure there runs a double range of quatrefoil
medallions, containing symbolic carvings in relief, bordered
by boldly defined mouldings (Plate 57). It is surprising that,

while the usual form of Gothic portal socle has a vertical
emphasis, at Amiens the socle extends from end to end of the
portal group in a broad, unbroken horizontal band, even
across the face of the buttress piers. An act of daring independence by the architect of a cathedral, which relies to a
notable extent for its expressive effect, almost exclusively
indeed, on verticals! But, for the portal group, Robert de
Luzarches reckoned on the imposing result which would be
produced by the strong contrast between the horizontal
treatment below and the soaring verticals above and, at the
same time, by the unifying function of the broad stone band
linking together the three portal bays. Any suggestion of
heaviness is avoided. It was here that the quatrefoil motif
assumed its commanding position in the vocabulary of
Gothic frame features, which it maintained well into the
early Italian Renaissance. The familiar competition panels
by Ghiberti and Brunelleschi for the new doors of the
Baptistery at Florence display the quatrefoil pattern.

The delicate precision with which this four-leaf sequence
is distributed over the socle at Amiens, each panel lightly
touching its neighbours above, below, and to the sides, is
admirably done, especially when we consider that these
horizontally arranged medallions are also axially related to
the monumental figures immediately above them. In many
cases this relationship is not only formal, for the panels are
used for representing ideas for which no more space was to
be found on the voussoirs. These could now be displayed to
perfection where they are most easily seen, witness the
Months and the Signs of the Zodiac.

Above the socle structure large figures rise in even ranks
along the portal sides, interrupted only by the doorways.
The doors are so wide that all three are divided in the middle
by a trumeau, which carries an appropriately important
figure to form a perfect focal point for the portal bay. In the
centre is Christ; in the portal to the right stands Mary with
the Child; to the left, St. Firmin, first bishop of Amiens.

In comparison with Chartres, we enter at Amiens a new
phase in the development of the Gothic monumental figure.
Confronted by these stern, well-rounded forms, one is

tempted to call them "statuesque", especially when one recalls the delicate, narrow-shouldered men of Chartres. The Amiens figures have acquired fullness and weight; they seem to stand more firmly and to have won for themselves a certain amount of elbow room (Plate 57)! Nevertheless, they remain column figures, standing out from the wall structure in a "salient" layer of space, each supported and surmounted by baldacchini. When we look at this great order extending evenly across all three portals, we can see that the sculpture conforms to the law of Gothic architecture—unending rows of verticals, as in the nave wall of the interior, but verticals, so to speak, in bodily form. This impression is further enhanced by the way in which, in all the diversity of detail applied to the draperies, it is generally the vertical folds which are the dominant features, their tubelike pleats being sharply emphasized by the chief master. The subjects vary from portal to portal, the meaning of the figures alters, the artists change, but the verticals remain. For the sculptor working under the direction of the architect the difficulty lay in equating the figure appropriate to the theme to the formal framework provided. Hence the perpetuation of frontality, the emphasis on uniform height, the disinclination to relate the figures to one another beyond what was strictly necessary, even when the meaning required it.

The Mother of God

All these aspects are linked with ideas developed from the general conception of the architect of the façade, to which the composition of the Virgin Portal is also subordinated. On the tympanum, as at Chartres, the central theme and group of three scenes represent the Death, Ascension and Crowning of Mary, accompanied on the voussoirs by choirs of angels and the ancestors of Mary. On the trumeau stands the Mother of God herself, with the Infant in her arms and her feet on the serpent (Plate 64). On either side, in the portal jambs, the Annunciation, Visitation, Presentation in the Temple, the Adoration of the Magi, Herod, Solomon and the Queen of Sheba are represented by separate figures of larger than life size (Plates 58 and 59). We previously found at Chartres that Gothic commemorated the groups of the Annunciation and Visitation as column figures on the jambs —an expression of the growing contemporary cult of the Virgin. The Adoration continues as a "picture" on the tympanum, but at Amiens the Three Kings are raised to the status of large figures. This commemoration of the life of Mary with such a strikingly complete representation of the chief figures is an indication of the significance of the Virgin Portal of Amiens.

The ceremonial appearance of the Mother of God demands our special attention. The abundance of Virgin figures produced during the later centuries of Gothic sculpture make it easy to forget the importance of the great Madonna statues in the portals of the classic cathedrals (Plate 64). Mary enthroned with the Infant Christ as a focus of worship had its place in the history of Western art since the early middle ages, but the standing figure of the Madonna did not begin her brilliant reign until the advent of the great Gothic cathedrals, when veneration for Mary was evidently concentrated upon this new creation. A new woman-image had now arrived, with divine attributes, to whom men could turn as to a mother. Her rôle as Queen of Heaven at the entrance of the cathedral was a Gothic invention, and the portal madonne of the thirteenth-century cathedrals of Northern France set a standard in conception, form and significance for the Virgin figures in other regions of France and the Western world. Their history can be studied in the cathedrals of Chartres, Amiens, Reims and Paris. On the trumeau of the Virgin Portal of Chartres there stands, it is true, not Mary, as one would expect, but her mother, St. Anne, who holds her little daughter in her arms. But, so far as appearances go, a Mary with the Christ Child would not have looked very different in this position. She is wrapped in clinging, gently swirling draperies, their fullness concealed by the drooping folds. This slender, gossamer light figure of a woman, mild, detached, contemplative, with its wonderfully delicate, liquid lines, is one of the most exquisitely sensitive examples of early thirteenth-century monumental sculpture.

The Madonna of Amiens, which dates from about fifteen years later, initiates the sequence of large standing Mary-figures with the Infant Jesus in their arms. She, too, is visualized as the Queen of Heaven, Biblical associations being depicted by the serpent at her feet and the story of Eve on the socle. She wears a long flowing gown and a mantle over her shoulders, which is gathered up in front and over the left forearm. The feet of the Christ Child are supported in the cross folds of this mantle, which remained a motif common to every figure of Mary in the classic cathedrals of the thirteenth century.

In comparison with Anne of Chartres we can detect in Mary of Amiens a greater feeling for the shape of the body. Gone are the charming reticence and self-effacement conveyed by the figure of St. Anne. The upper part of the body is firmly modelled. The gestures and grasp of the Child's hands are shown. The clear, full, symmetrical lines of the face reflect the ideal conception of beauty of High Gothic. The glance of the Madonna, like that of the Infant Jesus—He is in the act of blessing—is directed straight at the worshipping populace.

The Madonna on the middle portal of the west front at Reims, depicted also as the Queen of Heaven (Plate 65), dates from about ten years later. She is placed in the most important position, precisely on the axis of the cathedral, of which she is the patroness. In type, the figure resembles the Mary of Amiens, but there are clear signs of a change in conception. The sublime aloofness of the Amiens Madonna has yielded to an expression of amiability, although the effect is unhappily impaired by the badly executed head of the Christ Child. Mary's head is slightly turned, and a faint smile plays over her lips and in her eyes. The drapery with its swirling folds is dramatically handled, as at Amiens. Enveloping the figure from below is a splendid cloak, its folds gathered in a single tuck under Mary's left arm. The contrast between these voluminous folds and the close-fitting drapery above contributes to the impression of untrammelled movement. The remarkable opportunities for artistic expression and the wide possibilities for producing a monumental effect which existed merely in the arrangement of the folds of such draperies can easily be appreciated. If we also take into consideration two further, and later, portal Madonnas, the Virgin of the south transept of Amiens, celebrated as the "Vierge dorée (Plate 66), and the Virgin of the north transept façade of Paris (*circa* 1260) (Plate 67), we shall see how the outward form of the highest conception of womanhood personified in the Madonna had evolved in the thirteenth century and how important as models for the entire Western world were these figures created in the site workshops of French High Gothic. Those features which characterize the Madonna of Reims have now been enriched. In the "Golden Virgin" of Amiens the crowned Queen of Heaven turns to her Child with a smile, and this motherly touch is combined with a regal bearing. At the same time, while subordinating the drapery to the major features its dramatic possibilities are increased by a new emphasis on texture in the hang of the mantle and by a novel graduated draping of the folds.

The grace, elegance even, with which the great masters of the thirteenth century were able to endow this queenly figure, who is always portrayed in an easy standing attitude, is apparent in the Virgin of the north portal in Paris. From head to foot, the statue rises in one unbroken line, a movement of sublime nobility. The slight withdrawing motion of the upper part of the body and the corresponding lift of the head are inspired by the Madonna raising the Child shoulder high and taking one step back. The treatment of the mantle, with its flowing upward lines and differing response to the still and moving limbs, is superb.

In this unique series of Madonna figures is reflected more than an episode in the history of veneration for the Virgin. The developments which took place corresponded also to changes of theory in Gothic monumental figure sculpture, which must be taken into account when we turn now to the groups of figures on the Virgin Portal at Reims. For at Reims, too, the standing Madonna on the trumeau is accompanied on either side by scenes from her life recorded on the portal jambs, but in a manner which differs from Chartres and Amiens.

The Monumental Sculpture of Reims

The place in art history occupied by the monumental sculpture of Reims is conspicuously different from that of the two other cathedrals. This is primarily due to the fact that, in the course of the operation of building the cathedral, which—unlike Chartres and Amiens—was conducted from east to west (begun in 1211), a change of plan involved the lengthening of the nave by three bays, while a west front, already in part begun, gave place to a much richer and grander conception. This occurred soon after the transept portals and porches at Chartres had been extended and after Robert de Luzarches had started work on his cathedral in 1220 with the gigantic portal composition at the west end of the building. Clear evidence of the change of plan at Reims is provided by the two portals of the north transept façade, which were not in the first instance intended for that position, but for the west front of the original scheme. After the new project for lengthening the nave and for a west portal designed as a single unit to achieve a majestic effect, the older portals, already partly finished in the site workshops, consisting of a Last Judgment Portal and one dedicated to local saints (Sixtus Portal), were placed against the north transept façade, which was originally planned without a monumental entrance.

Another reason why the monumental sculpture of Reims occupies quite another place in art history is the different character of the site workshops, although it is difficult to describe what precisely this implied. In speaking of the classic cathedrals as a building type of a special kind, distinguished by a fundamental artistic quality, not to be explained by their architectural or stylistic history, but by a particular attitude in the craftsmen's lodges towards art, this different character is not least apparent in the sculpture which decorates the cathedrals. For example, when we refer to the dominance of the architect in the design of the west portal of Amiens, everybody understands what is meant, in the general sense, that architecture was regarded in Gothic as the principal art, and also that sculpture, as we have noted above, was subservient to the laws of predetermined architectural form. This is not the case with the cathedral of Reims, as Wilhelm Vöge clearly perceived. "At Reims the spirit of sculpture was in the air", he declared. "It inspired the architecture of the cathedral." It was the genius loci of the site workshops of Reims, where "a furnace of intensive creative energy" (Lethaby) made sculpture the first consideration. The west portals are compounded of an extraordinary wealth of sculptured figures, while the façade offers a wall of statuary to the nave interior. Nowhere is sculpture allotted so much space as at Reims, and nowhere else were to be found this concourse of master sculptors, individually distinguishable by their originality, qualities as artists and peculiarities of style. An account of High Gothic sculpture in France would inevitably take as its central theme the sculpture of Reims Cathedral and the prodigious variety of its manifestations. But here there arise problems of art history, for the chronology of this multitude of figures is still disputed by scholars. The jamb figures of the Virgin Portal also pose a number of special questions about the artistic aims of the chief master.

The portal architecture of the west front of Reims strives to embrace the whole façade with the effect of the decoration, which in its uniformity surpasses even the portal group at Amiens. The basic idea of amalgamating the buttress piers with the jambs of the portals remains unaltered. But while at Amiens the gables are set flush between the buttresses, at Reims they are thrust farther forward, so that they meet at a sharp angle in front of them. As the portal arch motif with the gable is also transferred to the outer face of the buttress pier, the result is a zigzag line of gables rising from the outside towards the middle, which, combined with the uninterrupted sequence of the portal jambs, produces a superb effect of unity.

One feature peculiar to Reims Cathedral is the treatment

of the tympana, all three of which are pierced by tracery windows. The sculptural embellishment which one would expect here for the Virgin Portal, Mary's Coronation, is raised to the panel over the portal, just beneath the gable. Only on the lintel, which was replaced in 1802 by the present inscription, do we find scenes from Mary's life, corresponding to the handling of the lintels on the side portals.

The architectural proportions of the portal elevations also differ from those of Amiens. It was possible at Reims to make the socle lower (Plate 42). The master decorated it throughout with the same drapery pattern. The monumental figures stand lower also, and, therefore, closer to the worshipper as he enters. In comparison with Amiens, the rows of capitals and baldacchini have exchanged their functions to advantage. At Reims the baldacchini are treated as a continuous chain of small gables, which emphasize very effectively the line from which the portal arches spring, while at the same time contributing to the clarity of the construction and providing comfortable space for the jamb figures.

The Virgin Portal of Reims and "the Master of Joseph"

In the jambs of the Virgin Portal stand four column figures on both sides; to the left of Mary arranged in pairs, to the right as a group of four (Plate 43 ff.). The Annunciation and Visitation in a group of two was a recognized treatment of the theme. We have already seen it in the north portal of Chartres and later at Amiens. The Presentation in the Temple, with the addition of Joseph and Hanna, forming a group of four, is an iconographical novelty. At Amiens we find only Mary and the high priest next to one another. At Reims they are flanked by Joseph and Hanna, who are obviously looking towards the middle. An unusual feature of this portrayal of an episode from Mary's life is that the figures, so closely associated in subject, appear to differ widely in stylistic character. It would not, of course, be unusual to be able to distinguish the hands of several artists —albeit under the direction of a master in chief—in the sculpture of a single portal. For example, this occurs in the Virgin Portal at Chartres. Differences, too, between a master and his assistants, uneven standards of artistic quality, that is to say, of a work supervised by a master, can be found in plenty. In the Virgin Portal of Reims, however, figures which are highly accomplished sculpture, but completely different in style, stand next to one another. The Mary of the Annunciation, with the severe lines of her drapery, is in striking contrast to the slim, youthful Gabriel in vigorously modelled robes who looks down upon her. The style exemplified in Mary we recognize as the vernacular idiom of the cathedrals of Paris and Amiens. But with the Angel of the Annunciation there enters a new manner in figure sculpture and this has come to be known as the Master of Joseph style, from the statue of Joseph, about which more will be said. Near the Annunciation Mary and Elizabeth form a Visitation group; both women are the work of the same hand, but differing in every respect from the adjacent Annunciation. A stanza of classical Latin has found its way here into the story of Mary's life. The beauty and accomplished artistry of this Visitation group have often been praised. Among Gothic artists, the master responsible for this work came closer than any to the sculpture of classical antiquity. (The chief master-sculptor of Bamberg Cathedral saw it and translated it into the cruder language of his own art.) That there was a sculptor in the site workshops of Reims Cathedral capable of creating such a figure of the Virgin, in which the spirit of Gothic merges with the classical, in which the texture of the exquisite folds of drapery and mantle contributes brilliantly to the expression of physical movement, and in which the head in outline and proportion portrays such an extraordinary measure of spiritual beauty in a woman's face, is one of the miracles which the genius loci of Reims provides for us.

On the opposite side stand Mary and the high priest, figures interpreted in the severe idiom of Amiens, between two statues by the Master of Joseph. This master, who created the Angel of the Annunciation, introduced an entirely new conception into figure sculpture, which was

marked by slender proportions, a new style of drapery,
lively gestures and a profoundly sympathetic facial expression. In the sculpture of Reims the smile, and it has many
different forms, rises to such a level of transcendent importance that the Master of Joseph invests the entire figure of
the Angel of the Annunciation, as well as those of the angels
flanking St. Nicaise (on the left-hand portal), with an
inspiring smile of hope; further evidence of the beneficent
spirit of the Biblical world in Gothic art.

But how can the striking juxtaposition of such varied
styles of figure sculpture in the Virgin Portal be explained,
especially when we still have to take into consideration the
Madonna on the trumeau? Is this juxtaposition a matter of
chronology, or is it the accidental outcome of being placed
there one by one? In the curious way in which these figures
are assembled there obviously lay a deliberate artistic intention on the chief sculptor's part; for the astonishing thing is
that the supervising master used the variety of styles to
express the variety in character of the figures. The humility,
modesty and shyness of the "handmaid of the Lord" at the
Annunciation could not have been more sensitively interpreted than in the simple, severe "style amiénois". The
joyful greeting of the heavenly messenger, the angel Gabriel,
could not have been more compellingly presented than with
that light, winged figure by the Master of Joseph. The
dignity and grace in the meeting of the two saints, Mary and
Elizabeth, have never been more nobly expressed in Western
monumental sculpture than in the inspiring tones of classical
antiquity at Reims. In the case of Joseph opposite, the man
of the world demeanour of the statue hardly corresponds
with our conception of Mary's husband, but the eager
interest of Joseph and Hanna in what is going on in their
midst gives the Presentation in the Temple a pleasant ceremonial air, unique in the monumental sculpture of the
time. Moreover, the manner in which the figures are composed in relation to one another leaves no doubt that Joseph
and Hanna were intended for the rôle which they are still
playing in this quartette. But were Mary and the high priest
designed for it as well?

For the art historian differences of style within a defined field normally mean differences of time. But a difficulty arises in accounting for the impressions conveyed by the Virgin Portal which are of such intense interest artistically. The style of the master of the Visitation, like the Paris-Amiens style, is older than that of the Master of Joseph, for we are able to study it in its original form before the Master of Joseph appeared. It would, therefore, be conceivable that the Master of Joseph, as the man responsible for designing the Virgin Portal for the new west front, made use of a collection of statues already available in the site workshops and gave them his own finishing touches. In the right-hand side portal he also incorporated the series of prophets, belonging to the older style, in his scheme of ornamental sculpture. A recent observer, Hamann McLean, has indeed expressed the view that the jamb figures of the Virgin Portal were commissioned at almost the same time (*Kunstchronik*, 1956, p. 288). Certainly there was no lack of high sculptural talent in the building workshops of Reims Cathedral. But, for a leading master to employ different styles to endow his figures and figure groups with particular qualities of mood and expression, appropriate to the incidents which they portray, is a singular commentary on the art of this period.

The Last Judgment—Chartres

In Gothic monumental sculpture the representation of the Last Judgment on the middle portal of the south transept façade at Chartres established an iconographical standard which, in its principal features, with certain incidental variations, is repeated in both the other great cathedrals (Plate 23). On the middle of the tympanum, the divine significance of the scene emphasized by the enveloping wisps of cloud, the enthroned figure of Christ sits in judgment on mankind, with His hands upraised and breast laid bare, so that His wounds may bear witness to His sufferings for the world (Plate 24). About His head attendant angels hold the instruments of the Passion: the cross, the crown of thorns, and the nails. On His right and left sit the Virgin and St. John, turning towards Him in intercession. In each corner an angel kneels, one holding the spear, the other the cross and the scourge. On the lintel the verdict is carried out. In the middle stands the Archangel Michael, and in his hands the scales, upon which the destinies of eternal damnation or eternal bliss are weighed. To his right an angel leads the chosen to paradise, while on his left devils drag the wicked down into the flames of hell. On both sides representatives can be seen of "all sorts and conditions of men": kings, bishops, gentlewomen, monks. The succession of figures continues on to the lower voussoirs. On the side of the damned we find a noble lady, a nun, a miser with his bulging bag of money, and a naked prostitute, each led by a grotesque devil. On the other side the blessed are on their way to paradise, which in mediaeval symbolism is depicted as Abraham's bosom, where their souls are seated in the guise of tiny human figures. The Resurrection of the Dead, rising from their box-like coffins, shows the first stage in the drama of the end of the world and occupies the next layer of voussoirs above. Over them are disposed the entire hierarchy of the heavenly host: Seraphim, Cherubim, Thrones, Dominations, Principalities, Powers, Virtues, Angels and Archangels.

On the trumeau (Plate 25), and, therefore, on the axis of the whole transept façade, stands Christ the Mediator, with right hand raised, and the lion and dragon under His feet (Psalm 91): "super aspidem et basiliscum ambulabis, conculcabis leonem et draconem." "Thou shalt go upon the lion and adder; the young lion and the dragon shalt thou tread under thy feet." Along the jambs and supported on small figures, stand Christ's witnesses, the twelve Apostles (who were never absent from mediaeval representations of the Last Judgment), with St. Peter and St. Paul at their head.

If we compare twelfth-century versions of the Last Judgment with their Apocalyptic visions, or the one at St. Denis, in which an acceptable iconographical representation first appeared in Gothic sculpture, we can instantly see that at Chartres an entirely new, clear and deeply fervent rendering of this powerful theme is given, and that the particular merit of this majestic composition of the Last Things far exceeds that of a mere prosaic imparting of information. Apart from this the south façade of Chartres, in comparison with the north front, is conspicuous for a firmer comprehension of the structural relationship between architecture and sculpture. Here the art lay above all in bringing the familiar theme convincingly to life while investing it with spiritual and devotional significance. The harmony of the architecture of façade and portal with the sculpture is complete. Verticals dominate even in the design of the figures, in the pose of the upraised arms of Christ, and the strict regimentation on the lintel of the Blessed and the Damned. This is equally true of the Apostles on the jambs (Plate 26), in which the aim is rather to depict a general type than individuals. The composition of the whole is the decisive factor. The Apostles are not conceived as personalities as they were in the post-mediaeval period, but only in their capacity as attendants upon Christ. Certainly, they are identifiable, but only by the attributes proper to them. Only Peter and Paul are recognizable by definite iconographical characteristics in the treatment of the head. It was a principle of mediaeval thinking to represent the tenets of belief, spiritual forces and historical values by rows of similar symbolic figures. A single idea could be varied, but its particular character was not differentiated. The number was more important than the significance of the individual conception, even though in the classic cathedrals certain changes took place. The master of the Last Judgment Portal at Chartres understood how to give the apostle-figures the degree of expressiveness demanded by the imposing architecture without allowing the architecture to overwhelm the sculpture.

The mediaeval believer found in the cathedrals not only visible evidence of the ordeal which confronted him at the Last Judgment, but of the battle that he had to wage during his life on earth before facing the Day of Judgment. It was an internal struggle between good and evil, a battle of the soul, which as early as the fourth century Aurelius Prudentius in his *Psychomachia* had described as a conflict between beings personifying the virtues and vices. Personifications of this kind were familiar to the entire middle ages, and were also adopted by the plastic arts, the virtues being represented as females and the vices in various forms. The original classification contained three theological virtues (faith, hope, charity) and four cardinal virtues (prudentia, fortitudo, justitia, temperantia). In opposition were seven vices. But such divisions were modified in the course of the middle ages. On the great cathedrals in the Gothic period twelve virtues and vices are opposed, at Chartres on the jambs of the porch in front of the Last Judgment Portal, and at Amiens in the relief pattern of the socle. At Reims the cycle is incomplete. They are no longer conceived as in conflict with one another, but are depicted in character, the virtues as girls holding a shield with various symbols, the vices in a dramatic scene with, for instance, despair taking its own life, cowardice as a knight fleeing from a hare, hardheartedness as a noble lady kicking a servant, inconstancy as a monk escaping from the cloister.

The Last Judgment—Amiens

The Last Judgment of the central portal of the west front at Amiens (Plate 60) has larger dimensions and more elaborate figure sculpture than at Chartres. The iconographical type is the same, only the spatial organization of the scenes and the style of presentation being changed. The tympanum is divided into three bands. On the lowest the dead are seen rising from the tomb, with the angel summoning them to judgment. In the middle stands the Archangel Michael with the scales. On the second band are the Blessed and the Damned, while above, on the third, under the baldacchino Christ sits in judgment, displaying His wounds, with John and Mary on either side, and the angel with the instruments of the Passion. Over this, at the pointed top of the tympanum, hovers the Christ of the Revelation, "and out of His mouth goeth a sharp sword". Upon the six rows of voussoirs are disposed, besides the scenes which, as at Chartres, are concerned with the separation of the Blessed and the Damned, all those who in the theological and ecclesiastical thinking of the time were gathered about Christ as the centre of the faith—martyrs, confessors, holy women, the elders of the Apocalypse, the tree of Jesse, the patriarchs of the Old Testament. Similar cycles are also found at Chartres, but in other positions corresponding to the differing architecture of portals and porches.

On the portal jambs, to the left and right, we see the parable of the wise and foolish virgins, five on each side. This parable had belonged from early Christian times to the repertoire of eschatological themes. Ten was the number given by Jesus (Matthew xxv):

"1. Then shall the kingdom of heaven be likened unto ten virgins, which took their lamps, and went forth to meet the bridegroom.

2. And five of them were wise, and five were foolish.

3. They that were foolish took their lamps, and took no oil with them.

4. But the wise took oil in their vessels with their lamps.

5. While the bridegroom tarried, they all slumbered and slept.

6. And at midnight there was a cry made, Behold the bridegroom cometh; go ye out to meet him.

7. Then all those virgins arose, and trimmed their lamps.

8. And the foolish said unto the wise, Give us of your oil; for our lamps are gone out.

9. But the wise answered, saying, Not so; lest there be not enough for us and you: but go ye rather to them that sell, and buy for yourselves.

10. And while they went to buy, the bridegroom came; and they that were ready went in with him to the marriage: and the door was shut.

11. Afterward came also the other virgins, saying, Lord, Lord, open to us.

12. But He answered and said, Verily I say unto you, I know you not.

13. Watch, therefore, for ye know neither the day nor the hour wherein the Son of Man cometh."

11—HG

Gothic incorporated this parable in its vocabulary of sculpture and, as an edifying illustration of the admonition to prepare for the day of decision and to keep the lamps always filled, linked it closely with the theme of the Last Judgment. At Chartres it is used on the voussoirs of the left-hand portal of the north front, as well as on the porch of the Last Judgment Portal of the south transept. In Paris the wise and foolish virgins are found on the restored jambs of Notre-Dame in an arrangement similar to Amiens. The wise virgins stand with their full lamps held in the air, while the foolish are distinguishable by their lamps pointed towards the ground and their gloomy expressions. In German thirteenth-century sculpture they provide a constantly recurring subject of monumental statuary.

On each side of the Last Judgment Portal at Amiens, six apostles are placed against the jambs (Plate 57). We have already discussed their formal qualities as sculpture and architectural relationship. In comparison with the Virgin Portal, the even ranks show more lively variations in the basic form, especially in the St. Paul sequence, thanks to differences in the pose of the head, size of the figures and movement in the drapery. Their attributes and the manner in which they are carried had a part to play in this, but most of these have been restored and given additions, so that their formal significance can no longer be judged. At Chartres the attributes enhance the general aspect of the figures by their greater purity of style.

The "mediating" Christ of the Amiens portal tramples upon a dragon and a lion, as at Chartres (Plates 61 and 62). In this figure-type of Christ the Mediator—an entirely French conception—the ideal of beauty of French High Gothic for the form of the head of Christ found perfect expression. There is something classical in the purity of the lines of the face, in the profile of the nose and of the eye-brows, which repeat the curve of the parted hair, and in the interpretation of the clear eyes with the straight horizontal line of the lower lids. The slightly arched mouth and curled beard add to the impression of complete repose.

The Last Judgment—Reims

The third "Beau Dieu", as the French call this type, stands at the Last Judgment Portal of Reims Cathedral (Plate 38), and we might well be confronted by a late classical figure, so completely does it differ from the strict, stylized attitude of the Christ of Chartres and the hovering posture of the Christ of Amiens. At Reims we can justifiably use the term "statuesque". The figure clearly differentiates in its pose between the leg bending in movement and the leg which is still, the treatment of the drapery eloquently expressing the physical action of standing. In its formal idiom this Christ-figure reflects the classical current in the monumental sculpture of Reims, which we have previously met in the work of the master of the Visitation on the Virgin Portal of the west front, and which is characteristic of a group of sculpture from the workshops of this cathedral. This classical element seems to have been a regional matter, for since Carolingian times Reims had been particularly receptive to late classical influences through the art of the monastery schools. But a primarily local manifestation of style at the time of the building of the cathedrals, which was certainly stimulated by the many Gallo-Roman monuments still surviving, combined with a more general tendency, widely noticeable in early thirteenth-century Western art, to keep eyes and minds alert for the outward forms of classical antiquity. The most striking example of this is provided by the court art of the Emperor Frederick II in Southern Italy. For the development of Gothic monumental sculpture in Reims Cathedral, this readiness to turn to classical models meant an endeavour to achieve a less artificially posed and more human interpretation of the Christ-figure.

The almost classical bearing of the "Beau Dieu" of Reims, however, does not imply that the development of monumental sculpture at Reims was to proceed on similar lines. The Master of Joseph represented a Gothic counter-tendency. In describing the Joseph on the Virgin Portal (Plate 49), we cannot use the terminology which we needed for the Beau Dieu. Joseph's silhouette is narrow at the bottom, broadens out towards the elbows in billowing folds of drapery and tapers again past slender shoulders to the pointed cap. This master introduced a more Gothic demeanour, "a challenging liveliness" (Vöge), but not without certain traces of classicism appearing in a few figures. Once again it is astonishing to see how the sculptor, with his sure artistic perception, was able to choose a definite style appropriate to the expression of particular qualities in the figure without falling into eclecticism. The formal vocabulary of "Joseph" would not have been suitable for creating a "Beau Dieu". In order to ensure that Christ the Mediator should reflect the dignity and firmness of presence, the magnitude in conception and unity of design, suitable to a statue occupying the central position on the Last Judgment Portal, a classical, Roman vocabulary was selected. The site workshops of Reims disclose more varied prowess in their sculpture than the other great cathedrals.

Dramatic Characterization

At Reims we can appreciate the variety of artistic possibilities which Gothic had created for the theme of the Last Judgment in a relatively short space of time. Owing to changes in plans during the building of the cathedral, the Last Judgment Portal at Reims was not completed and does not display such uniformity of treatment as those at Chartres and Amiens. In time it occupies, so far as its principal features are concerned, a middle position between the other two cathedrals. In conception and execution it displays an entirely different spirit, a freedom in composition and a departure from rigid figure sequences, which result in a new and highly dramatic representation of the theme. On the double band (panel) which depicts the dead rising from their stone coffins (Plate 34) the sculptor offers abundant evidence of his mastery of the physical movements of naked bodies—rising, bending, climbing, turning, leaning—some with their backs bared and some wrapped in shrouds. The composition of the lowest band, in the middle of which, instead of the angel with the scales, a baldacchino was placed for the figure of Christ (subsequently added), two scenes, treated as separate compositions, point the contrast between paradise and the procession of the wicked being dragged down to hell. On the side of paradise, angels carry souls, depicted as tiny human figures, to an enthroned Abraham, in whose bosom they will find repose. On the other side we see a group of the damned, bound together with an iron chain held by a devil, the representatives of different classes and callings being distinguished by remarkably vivid characterization. Hell is shown, on the right, as a huge cauldron set upon a blazing fire, in which their souls are tortured.

At the top of the tympanum, and also forming part of the Last Judgment group, there occurs an incident of intense drama. Mary and John (the Baptist, not the Evangelist) turn in passionate entreaty to Christ, a complete contrast to the solemn restraint of their attitude at Chartres.

The vitality, which is so clearly expressed in the handling of the tympanum, dominates in various degrees other parts of the portal as well. The supreme artistry of the master is apparent in the two Apostles, Peter and Paul, standing on either side of the entrance. Both figures (Plates 37 and 39) reveal once again the outstanding sculptural talent available on the site workshops at Reims at the time when the cathedral was beginning to rise. Wilhelm Vöge, with his reliable critical eye, was the first to recognize these Apostles as masterpieces.[1] But he only laid stress on their "naturalism", on those characteristics which set them apart from other contemporary figures and from the four other Apostles of the same portal. It is essential to add, however, that with these figures of St. Peter and St. Paul a completely new image of man grew up in the shadow of the cathedral, an image unknown to the pre-Gothic art of the West. The early middle ages had used the human form only as a figure physically and spiritually of one dimension for the art of religious expression. In the evolution of Gothic this figure acquired both physical and psychological dimensions, and, in the process, opened up entirely new artistic possibilities. A remarkable advance had taken place in a century from the

[1] W. Vöge, *Die Bahnbrecher* . . . Ztschr. f. bildende Künst, 1913-1914.

portal figures of Moissac to the Last Judgment at Reims. The Peter of Moissac is still early mediaeval mime in sculpture, modelled in almost convulsive movement and seemingly pressed by an invisible force against the wall, an item in the symbolic paraphernalia for inspiring fervour. With the Peter of Reims a transformation has taken place in Gothic art. This Peter is carved in the round, as a free-standing figure beneath a canopy. The structure of the body can be seen. Although still a High Gothic column figure, the statue is conceived from within and expresses Peter's personality. The head is boldly modelled and the face combines energy, wisdom and thoughtfulness (Plate 40). We recognize at once that the sculptor has drawn his standards from life, and the same is true of the figure of Paul (Plate 41). Here also we find a personality with definite characteristics of mind and temperament, conceived from an entirely different stand-point. It is remarkable to see how the artist has introduced genuine qualities of character into the traditional, stylized, outward marks of the chief Apostles—the short curly hair and beard of Peter, the high forehead and longer, full beard of Paul. The gaze of St. Paul is directed high and far into the distance. St. Peter's eyes are upon his immediate surroundings, ready to act in a moment.

A World Below and a World Above

These radical changes of approach to monumental sculpture can be followed in all their stages on the transept façades, as well as on the Last Judgment Portal and the figures of kings on the buttress piers of the rose storey. The sculptural embellishment of Reims Cathedral extends far beyond the immediate area of the portals; indeed it begins with the figures of angels outside the chevet chapels. On the rose tier, above the Last Judgment, space is provided for a further group of sculpture which also embraces a completely separate theme. The voussoirs framing the rose recount the story of Adam and Eve, and how they brought sin into the world. By the side of the rose they appear as full size statues with long draperies. (They were first used as monumental figures in the nude at Bamberg Cathedral.) In the corresponding position next to the rose of the south transept stand figures impersonating the Old and New Testaments, Synagogue and Ecclesia, with which so much theological teaching was associated. In Paris they are set on the buttress piers of the west portals, but at Chartres they have not survived, and they do not occur at all at Amiens. Those at Strasbourg and Bamberg reach a high level of artistic perfection and are also linked with the eschatological theme cycle. They reveal a rich sensuous gusto.

The middle ages demanded of man that he should live always in the spirit. Nothing was conceivable or intelligible except from the viewpoint of a world below subordinated to a transcendent world above. But this lofty ideal was combined with the practical aspiration to bring this supernatural world within tangible reach of human experience and so make it accessible to the material world. This is exactly what occurred in the classic Gothic cathedrals, as we have seen in countless manifestations of monumental sculpture.

The changing relationship of sculpture to architecture in the three cathedrals is grounded in changing conceptions of art. At Chartres the Apostles occupy the jambs of the Last Judgment Portal (Plate 26), where they contribute an imposing solemnity to the theological lessons conveyed by the scheme of ideas as a whole. The figures are thus employed as an architectural device at the expense of their interest as individual representations. At Reims the master of Peter and Paul has moved forward, and shows that the sculptor was now striving for independence in his attitude to architecture, to explore new facets of personality in presenting a noble interpretation of the human race. Here were laid the foundations of Western art and the bonds released from stylized form, without which neither Sluter, Donatello, Michelangelo, nor the sculptors of German late Gothic altars or the master carvers of the Baroque, would be thinkable.

Saints' Portals

In an appraisal of the sculptural achievements of High Gothic and of the problems of style formation, the Martyrs' portals of the great cathedrals occupy a position similar to those portal types which we have already discussed. But in subject matter they broaden our view of what was considered worthy of presentation in the thirteenth century, and they produced a series of "saint types" in monumental sculpture of high artistic merit.

In the programme on the south front of Chartres Cathedral, of which Christ is the central theme, martyrs and confessors are ranged on both sides of the Last Judgment Portal. The left side-portal, which is of lower quality artistically, is dedicated to the martyrs, who bore witness to Christ by their death. On the lintel is depicted the stoning of St. Stephen; on the tympanum Christ appears as a standing figure; the voussoirs are devoted to various themes; on the jambs four saints are placed on either side to form column figures, while the side piers of the porches carry panels of relief recording the sufferings of the martyrs. Of the large figures, the two outermost, St. George and St. Theodore, are particularly striking. They belong to a later date than the stiffer, more typical column figures next to them, and illustrate the new naturalism which monumental sculpture was striving to achieve in the 1220s. Both wear the chain-mail and long tunic, and carry the weapons, of knights of the period, illustrating the ideals of chivalry and noble bearing admired in the thirteenth century.

The portal to the right introduces us to the great confessors, among whom we meet two of the most popular saints, St. Martin and St. Nicholas. Their best-known deeds are told on the tympanum—St. Martin dividing his cloak for the beggar and St. Nicholas helping an impoverished gentleman, his neighbour. The latter is seen half-risen from his bed, his three daughters in lamentation behind him. The legend tells how the poor man, in his need, was about to drive his daughters "into open worldly sin", so that they could live on the proceeds of their shame. "When St. Nicholas heard this, he was horrified by this sinfulness; so he went away and wrapped a piece of gold in a cloth and cast it privily at night through a window of the poor man's house and departed again in secret." This favourite episode in mediaeval art is shown on the tympanum, with St. Nicholas standing outside the house in the act of throwing the bag of money through the window.

Both saints also appear as statues on the jambs, St. Martin with Jerome and Gregory the Great; St. Nicholas as a bishop, with Ambrose of Milan and Pope Leo. In these two groups of three figures the sculptor showed himself a true master in expressing the dignity, authority, hieratic magnificence and spiritual nobility of men who were a part of Church history and also revered as saints. In the Nicholas sequence he employs formal symmetry for the richly ornamented clerical robes, strict frontality, exaggerated proportions, and arms upraised three times in the same gesture of blessing, in order to give an impression of sublime solemnity. More movement is apparent on the other side. The two saints wearing tiara and mitre tower above bare-headed Jerome in the middle, who turns his head to one side and holds an open book in his hands.

On the axis of the north transept façade of Reims is placed a portal dedicated to local saints (Plate 50), and on the trumeau of its spacious doorway stands St. Sixtus, who brought Christianity to Champagne; the jambs, on one side, show St. Rémi as a bishop, accompanied by Clovis and an angel; on the other St. Nicaise, holding his head in his hands to symbolize his martyrdom. Next to him are his sister Eutropie, who shared his fate, and an angel proclaiming their triumph and eternal salvation. On the wide tympanum the deeds and miracles of both saints, Rémi and Nicaise, are recounted in detail with figures and scenes, which are deployed more or less evenly over superimposed ribbon-like panels.

The rôle played by St. Sixte (Sixtus) in Champagne fell in Picardy to the lot of St. Firmin, first bishop of Amiens. The latter occupies the place of honour on the trumeau of the left side-portal of the west front of Amiens Cathedral. The tympanum, also devoted to him, depicts, in a manner suggesting an illuminated missal rather than sculpture, the discovery of the saint's body and the removal of his relics to Amiens. The monumental figures on the jambs (bishops, martyrs, saints—among them a woman, St. Ulphe—and angels) reflect in their arrangement the paratactic principle followed on the other two portals and exemplify, with the exception of St. Ulphe, the stiff formal idiom which, allowing for stylistic variations, is typical of Amiens.

About half a generation after the Sixtus Portal, the workshops of Reims Cathedral took up once again the theme of the Saints' Portal for the west front, under the direction of the Master of Joseph. The difference is marked. St. Nicaise now stands between two angels smiling at him and announcing the victory of heaven (Plate 51), a great advance in expressive treatment over the earlier portal. The other figures, both women and men, reveal a similar change in conception, while refinements in details of style make it possible to give each statue the individual personal qualities of the saint which it represents, as well as the features of an elevated interpretation of the human race, so that they combine in creating, in the sublime composure of their demeanour, a true *civitas coelestis*.

9. MONUMENTAL STAINED GLASS

Luminous Space and Pageantry

THE EXTENT to which the reddish-violet light of Chartres Cathedral helps to produce an atmosphere of enchantment in the interior has already been mentioned. The huge clerestory windows, which the master-designer used as containing elements, serve like the windows of the side aisles and ambulatory not only as a means of translating the architecture into luminous space, but are also combined with a pictorial pageantry which profoundly affects the interior and supplies a decisive share of that sublime majesty characteristic of Gothic interior design. Would the impression be the same, we may ask, if the windows were glazed with plain coloured panes? Far from it. These pictures are an important factor. Even more than the statuary the figures in stained glass bring into direct experience the feeling of transcendence, for they are immaterial creatures of light, set like magically glowing symbols in the frontiers of space.

In its range and content this world of pageantry embraces far more than the sculpture. The sculptor's work is largely confined to the immediate area of the portals; the stained-glass artist's creations spread their influence into every part of the cathedral interior. Since High Gothic used glazed surfaces of unparalleled dimensions and filled them with the glorious company and splendid episodes of the Christian Church, with Christ, the Virgin Mary and the Saints, with their deeds, legends and miracles, with everything in fact which men needed to know and to believe, we can obtain from stained glass a valuable insight into the mentality of the thirteenth century.

Benefactors

Among the classic cathedrals, the stained glass of Chartres makes the most important contribution to our knowledge of the art. Amiens has lost its mediaeval glass, and at Reims only a small part survives, most of which is in the clerestory windows of the choir. Chartres compensates for these depredations by offering us an almost complete display of original glass. Of 186 window designs, 152 can be seen today, while records survive of those destroyed between the eleventh and eighteenth centuries. All these windows were endowed individually, and since the benefactors are identifiable by inscriptions and other indications, we are able to trace the part played by the whole population in the adornment of a great cathedral. Among those who endowed the stained glass were members of the royal house, Blanche de Castille, St. Louis of France, the Duc de Bretagne and others of his family. The Comte de Chartres and many of the nobility subscribed, as did the clergy and the guilds of tradesmen, bakers, butchers, clothiers, tanners, money changers, carpenters, vintners, spicers, smiths, water carriers, joiners, coopers, masons, shoemakers, armourers, weavers, skinners, turners, pastry-

cooks, innkeepers and others. As all these guilds are recorded
as benefactors by the portrayal of their professional activities
(on the lowest window panels), we also discover what was
considered typical of the crafts and trades. Whether, apart
from their contributions to the cost of decorating the church,
the benefactors had any closer connection with the subjects
depicted on the windows which they endowed, is not known.
It is reasonable to suppose that in many instances the patron
saints of the corporations are represented, but we do not
always know which patrons were chosen in the thirteenth
century. It is also apparent that several guilds honoured the
same saints as their protectors.

In allocating the endowments certain positions of conspicuous distinction were selected. These included the great
rose windows and lancets of the transept fronts, endowed by
the most prominent families, the north rose by the Queen
and Regent, Blanche de Castille; the south rose by the
family of Dreux-Bretagne, the head of which, Pierre
Mauclerc, had become Duke of Brittany. He and his wife,
Alix de Thouars, can be seen on the lower sections of the
lancets beneath the rose. The figures outside on the socle
of Christ the Mediator, on the south portal, represent the
same benefactors.

The clerestory windows of the choir, which are particularly
impressive, were endowed by the bakers, butchers, clothiers
and money changers, and also by a certain Gaufridus.

Themes

In subject matter also certain positions of greater significance
emerge from the general scheme of window embellishment.
The upper windows of the choir are dedicated to themes
associated with the Virgin. The middle one, on the axis of
the cathedral, presents, one above the other, the Annunciation, Visitation, and Mary enthroned with the Christ-child.
The adjacent windows show figures of Daniel, Jeremiah,
Moses, Isaiah, Aaron, Ezekiel and David.

The Madonna occupies the centre of the great north rose
as well, surrounded by ancestors and prophets. On the lancet

windows beneath, however, the principal figure is St. Anne with Mary in her arms, thus repeating the sculptural motif on the trumeau of the Virgin Portal. The St. Anne window is accompanied on either side with characters from the Old Testament: David, Solomon, Melchisedek and Aaron.

Opposite, on the south rose and its associated lancets, we find cycles from the New Testament. The rose itself is devoted to the veneration of the enthroned Christ in the middle. Deployed in concentric circles about this centre-piece are the Apocalyptic beasts, angels and twenty-four elders, as described in the Revelation of St. John. On the lancets under the rose stands the Mother of God as Queen of Heaven, with the Christ-child (in the act of blessing) in her arms. To the left and right, in a literal illustration of the theory that the evangelists rest upon the shoulders of the prophets and that the New Testament signifies the fulfilment of the Old, the four prophets are carrying the four evange-lists: Jeremiah supporting St. Luke; Isaiah, St. Matthew; Ezekiel, St. John; and Daniel, St. Mark.

Just as the west front opens outwards into a Christ portal, so its window wall on the inside is entirely devoted to Christ. The three great twelfth-century windows tell the story of Jesus, beginning on the left with the tree of Jesse. The middle window, in a densely packed sequence of tableaux, recounts the life of Our Lord from the Annunciation to the entry into Jerusalem (reading, as with all stained-glass windows, from the bottom upward). The third window contains the story of the Passion in twelve episodes, starting with a representation of the Transfiguration and ending with the incident at Emmaus. The great rose, with Christ as Judge at the centre, introduces the Last Judgment and conforms to the icono-graphy with which we are already familiar from the Judgment portal.

In the manner in which the most important events of the Bible are reflected on the rose fronts, the windows show a division of emphasis in subject matter similar to that of the portal sculpture. All the remaining windows of the clerestory and side aisles, with few exceptions, belong to the saints. For the most part, these appear on the windows of the upper nave as large figures floating one by one in a sea of coloured light, creatures of a dream world, sometimes bathed in a strange barbaric splendour, which seems to glow with an unearthly fire. The windows of the flanking aisles are not decorated with single figures, but with stories from the lives of the saints. The abundance of incidents which they recount can only be hinted at here. In the windows of Chartres we have a painted Legenda Aurea of the most impressive kind, earlier in date than the work of Jacobus de Voragine. These legends in pictures had the merit of being not merely told, but actually seen, and the vivid narrative possibilities of thirteenth-century stained glass brought into immediate visual experience a sense of translation to a higher world. Never subsequently in any comparable branch of the arts has the power of allegory been more brilliantly applied than in Gothic stained glass. Moreover, by the very nature of his art, the glass painter was able to go more deeply than the sculptor into the essence of the lesson which he had to convey.

The structural character of his windows, in particular, allowed him much more space. Let us take, by way of example, the legends of the two popular saints, Martin and Nicholas, whom we have previously met in the sculpture of the south transept portal. Admittedly they had at their disposal the dignity implicit in the monumental sculpture of a Saints' portal, but both had to be accommodated on the same tympanum with two scenes from their legends. In the interior an entire window (chevet chapel) was dedicated to St. Martin, and no less than three windows in various locations to St. Nicholas. On the Martin window, endowed by the shoemakers, both the scenes also occur which we have already noticed on the tympanum; the division of the cloak and the dream of St. Martin, when Christ appears to him with the cloak which he gave to the beggar. In addition, a further thirty-three glass panels are found on which episodes in St. Martin's life are told. It is the same with the three St. Nicholas windows, which are divided into a series of scenes.

An Overall Plan

With regard to the many points of identity in theme between the sculpture outside and the windows inside, the question as to whether the stained glass follows an overall iconographical programme has been variously answered. Delaporte and Mâle have denied it. W. Schöne has expressed the view that a complete correspondence between exterior and interior was intended at least in theory.[1] For proof we need not compare each individual figure and scene, but those "iconographical unities" which arise from associated ideas. Whether such proof can be extended to every part of this vast and comprehensive sequence of tableaux is uncertain. But it would be reasonable to expect that in the ordered universe of a cathedral every element which contributed to the whole, including the stained glass, would be subordinated to an overall plan.

Within the architectural scheme of the interior an overall plan for the glass clearly existed. It is apparent in the clerestory windows of the nave which, despite many different hands, are filled with large single figures out of a proper respect for distance, and in the aisle windows which, in contrast, display highly complex figure patterns.

In these exceptionally lofty legend windows the art of the glass painters lay in their capacity to organize coherently a dense concentration of incident, preserve the decorative unity of the whole, and invest everything with the mysterious power of translucent colours which are so conceived that they mutually reinforce and strengthen one another, blending finally into a sumptuous tapestry of austere, sensuous magnificence. Their artistic power and perfection depends upon a system as deliberately calculated and sublime in effect as the architecture or the portal sculpture. Just as High Gothic portal architecture imposed upon the sculptors a prescribed form, so for the glass painter the structure of the "armature" generally defined the form of a section of window (Fig. 49). The equipping of wide glazed surfaces with hand-wrought iron rods (armatures) meant originally no more

[1] W. Schöne, *Kunstchronik.* 1949. Page 205.

Fig. 49: CHARTRES. Stained Glass
Left: The Prodigal Son   *Right:* Legends of Charlemagne

than a functional arrangement of horizontals and verticals, as can still be seen in the twelfth-century windows of the west front of Chartres. But like Gothic buttress work which was first used only as a technical reinforcing device, the armatures for stained glass developed in the early thirteenth century into an art form. They provided not only, in a material sense, support for the panes; but, from the standpoint of design, this geometrically regular and symmetrically constructed lattice governed both the general organization of the whole composition and the detailed disposition of every part of the stories presented. Moreover, the pattern of the armatures varied from window to window, producing delightful new combinations of geometrical figures with squares, rhomboids, circles, semi-circles, segments, quatrefoils and so on. Behind this lattice work were constructed the coloured background, the lively ornamental patterns and multi-coloured scenes, which tell their stories according to the principle of coloured silhouettes, that is to say, without, if possible, obscuring the outlines at any point. There are many differences in the way in which composition and frame structure are adjusted to one another. The window may be very simply organized, as in the one dedicated to St. Chéron, where the iron rods divide the scheme into a series of tiers, on each of which the figures are set under painted arches. It is probably no mere chance that this particular window was endowed by the masons and sculptors, who may well have supplied the design from their own repertoire. A window, however, sometimes acquired a highly complicated base frame, as in the case of the St. Nicholas window, endowed by the apothecaries, with its quatrefoils crossed diagonally by the armatures. In the story of St. Sylvestre the glass painter subordinated the pose of the figures, the folds of the draperies, and the architecture of the scenes, to a strict verticality, which is maintained in opposition to the arch forms of the frame and the rhomboidal pattern of the background. If we want a yardstick to gauge the high skill of these glass painters in composition, we should study the window depicting the noble and exciting legend of St. Eustache, in which the delicate draughtsmanship of a miniature is combined with marked power of expression and a particularly apt arrangement of the figures. The composition on the lower rhomboidal panel showing St. Eustache (when he was still called Placidus) hunting, with riders, galloping horses, hunted stags and hunting hounds, is a masterpiece of the glass painter's art.

It would be impossible, however, to describe here the inexhaustible riches of this painted Legenda Aurea. But a word must be added about colour.

Colour

The three large twelfth-century windows of the west front of Chartres are particularly significant for the quality of their colour. This is characterized by a light blue ground of ethereal delicacy, which contrasts with the variegated patterns of the figures, the Jesse window being perhaps more brilliant in its effect than the other two. Viollet-le-Duc (who incidentally devoted a perspicacious article in his *Dictionary of Architecture* to the translucent stained glass of the twelfth and thirteenth centuries) compares the blue of these windows to an autumn sky and stresses this limpid ethereal quality of the twelfth-century colour. We become immediately aware of it as soon as we turn to the thirteenth-century windows. Blue and red are now the important tones. The blue background is darker, deeper and stronger, and the various tonal values are more positive and sharply contrasting.

At the same time in the thirteenth-century glass which gives Chartres Cathedral its characteristic light, there are considerable variations in colour effects, combined with divergences in pictorial style, explicable by chronological differences and by stylistic fashions in the workshops engaged in window embellishment. The lancet windows of the north transept are notable for greater areas of colour in stronger, but harsher, tones, which contrast with the exquisitely modulated windows of the nave clerestory.

The character of the colours flooding through the nave from the huge windows of the apse, in which the style of the figures illustrates a classical tendency in the treatment of the draperies, shows variations. It is brightest in the window portraying the enthroned Virgin. The darker tones of those on either side supply a contrast, in which a mixture of browns and yellows predominates, whilst the glass of the flanking sides of the polygon once again emphasizes more strongly the blue ground.

The sensuous power of the luminous tones of Chartres glass, which waxes and wanes in strength as the day proceeds, grows at dusk, when the windows seem to glide loose from the framework of the cathedral architecture and appear like colour floating in space.

According to dates given by Delaporte or which can be reliably inferred, all the windows were endowed and set in place during the period in which the cathedral was being built, a stupendous feat of creative and artistic prowess, apart from its extraordinary practical difficulties. "In the windows of this period the dominant colours, red and blue, and next to them, yellow and green (and even white and black), attained as primary phenomena the highest level of intensity known to the history of art."[1]

[1] W. Schöne, *Über das Licht in der Malerei*. Berlin, 1954. Page 42.

PART TWO

II.   ECCLESIA SPIRITUALIS

Evolution of the Church Visible

ECCLESIA MATERIALIS significat ecclesiam spiritualem."
"The material church signifies the spiritual church."
This sentence epitomizes the attitude of the mediaeval
theologian. The cathedral architect did not speculate about
its meaning. Villard de Honnecourt speaks in the notes and
inscriptions in his sketchbook only about the cathedral as a
building and of the art of the architect, not of the significance
of architectural forms. His practical intentions are precisely
stated at the beginning: "Villard de Honnecourt greets you
and begs all those who may use in their work the devices
which they find in this book to pray for his soul and remem-
ber him. For in this book good advice can be found on the
noble art of the mason, on the craft of carpentry, and . . . on
the uses of drawing which the study of geometry demands
and teaches."[1]

This does not mean that he knew nothing of the significance of forms, rather that this was obvious to him. On the
other hand, the mediaeval theologian tried to fit what was
tangible and apparent into the tenets of the Christian faith.
The visibility of the "ecclesia materialis" was a token of the
invisibility of the "ecclesia spiritualis". To him everything
was symbolic.

The sentence quoted above is so general in character that
it contains nothing with reference to the Gothic cathedral
which is not applicable to all forms of Christian church
building. It takes this as a simple fact without inquiring
about changes in its form in the course of centuries. The

[1] Hahnloser. Page 12.

mediaeval theologian recognized no differences in the "styles" or appearance of church construction, but only of types, whilst we, looking back through the evolution of history, can see that the appearance of the ecclesia materialis has constantly altered, although its teaching remains the same. We are also no longer inclined to recognize changes only in the technical design of the building. Architecture has always had something significant to say about the time and place in which it originated. The spirit creates the technique for doing this. The Christian Church in the West cannot point to one type of sacred building, and from this fact derives our conception of the succession of architectural styles stretching from early Christian church architecture to the end of the Baroque period. Ought we not to conclude from these changes that the ecclesia spiritualis has also changed? Undoubtedly we should do so, but we must also bear in mind that there are both immutable and mutable strata in the ecclesia spiritualis. The mysteries of the faith can be received in a variety of forms which reflect historical changes in the requirements of church services. The rich religious life expressed in changes of liturgical practice in the early middle ages suggests that changes in church building were to be understood as changes in the framework for worship.[1]

The possibility of change in the ecclesia spiritualis is revealed by the way in which particular aspects of Christian truth could at certain times be stressed and given prominence according to special religious needs. These accentuations can be explained from the viewpoint of changing devotional practice, as we have already shown in an earlier chapter with reference to the Elevation of the Host, a characteristic feature of Gothic liturgical procedure.

Mediaeval art history, moreover, makes it obvious that within the Christian communion the attitude of believers to the material and spiritual worlds did not remain the same throughout the centuries. Here art history can present a clearer view than mediaeval theology, for it has at its

---

[1] Cf. The genetic exposition of the (Roman) Mass in J. A. Jungmann. *Missarum Solemnia*. Vol. I. Vienna, 1948.

disposal the panorama of historical evidence in chronological perspective. It recognizes, for example, that changes
occurred in the forms in which the divine personality was
represented, and that different facets of the godhead were
symbolized at different times. As this was not a matter of
chance, but followed a definite historical pattern, we are
bound to conclude that Western religious art is an accurate
reflection of mankind's changing attitude to the spiritual
world.

Divine Truths in Visible Proximity

The possibility of changes in the conception of the form of
Christ is inherent in his dual nature of God and Man. An
alteration in the believer's attitude to the world above found
expression, for instance, in a greater emphasis upon the
divine or human side of Christ at particular periods. In the
early middle ages we see how art fulfilled the mission of
showing the supreme importance of a Biblical basis for man's
existence and of his binding acceptance of this aspect of the
Godhead. God and his world was the theme. Man, if he
appeared at all, was part of God's world.

In Gothic we find for the first time a clear change in the
symbolic conception of the Divine personality, which is
linked with the aim of religious art to bring to the believer
all the mystical truths of the faith in tangible, visible form.
For this the Gothic cathedral was the chosen theatre. In
addition, the form in which Christ was represented changed.
However strongly the divine aspect was brought out in the
monumental symbolism of the cathedral by Christ's central
place, both in the composition and in its theme, his human
side began to emerge for the first time. Men wanted to see
the image of Christ, not as a warning to the transgressor,
not as the supreme example of moral rectitude or as the
judge at the Last Judgment, but as the Saviour, who brought
consolation and who had suffered for mankind. He showed
his wounds and, in the repertoire of Gothic imagery, the
story of the Passion now assumed greater importance. In
Late Gothic we find Christ depicted as a man among men.

What held good for changes in the appearance of the form of Christ, was also true of all other subjects in Christian symbolism. They evolved. To some extent they were new creations. In the thirteenth century they were brought into closer contact with the congregation and more strikingly represented than in early periods. Gothic led to a new epoch of a symbolical interpretation of everything connected with the spirit, using imagery and allegory on a vast scale. The figures always express something else besides what is immediately noticeable on the surface. They constantly indicate wider associations. The expressive resources of allegory and symbolism in the visual arts of the middle ages, especially in Gothic cathedrals, lie in the metaphorical richness of the Bible and, in the case of the New Testament, in the parables of Jesus. A conspicuous example is provided by the parable of the wise and foolish virgins, which had travelled far along the road of the art of pictorial illustration before finding a secure position in the portal sculpture of the Gothic cathedral (for the first time on the west portal of the Abbey church of St. Denis).

The Sum of Belief and Knowledge

The symbolism of mediaeval art, however, derives from a great variety of sources, and not least from theological speculation.

The opportunities for expressing with a few figures, by the aid of allegory, symbolic representation, impersonation and typology, a wealth of meanings for those who understood how to "read" them, produced a complex mixture of past and future happenings on this earth, interpreted in a Christian sense, with an eye to the beginning and end of the world and to the road which Christ had to follow.

The "impersonations" of the Old and New Testaments, for instance, which we call "Synagogue" and "Ecclesia", gave tangible form by their attributes to the entire story of mankind's salvation. The extraordinary variety of allusion that was possible with two such figures, expressed in their relationship to the compositions in which they appear, has been recently set out in detail by Adolf Weis.[1] Mediaeval theologians never tired of referring to these associations. Moreover, there was nothing in the classic Gothic cathedrals which does not contain a deeper, esoteric significance. In fact, the Gothic cathedral with its sumptuous display of picture and narrative can be described for this point of view as the sum of everything which man at that time needed to know and to believe.

An indication of the variety of significance possible in certain Biblical incidents and their theological interpretation was given in the thirteenth century by Durandus, who systematized, in the mediaeval sense, his exposition in the following way. He deduced from the Holy Scriptures a fourfold meaning: historical, allegorical, tropological and anagogical. The first treats the story as literal fact. Next allegory gives to the text a sense which differs from that of the normal meaning of the words. Tropology, on the other hand, conveys a moral implication, interpretating the words (again somewhat differently from their everyday meaning) according to a moralistic viewpoint. The anagogical, which is closely linked with the allegorical, strove to find in the text a metaphysical connection either with the supramundane or with the church.[2]

Gradations of Meaning

During the post-mediaeval period all comprehension of the symbolic meaning of the (Gothic) pictorial arts disappeared; but, since the rediscovery of the middle ages in the nineteenth century, scholars have tried to disentangle once again the metaphorical significance of artistic expression in the mediaeval age and to find the sources from which interpretation is possible. In his book on the "Symbolik des Kirchengebaüdes", Joseph Sauer, with particular reference to older researches, has pointed out the range and peculiar

[1] Adolf Weis, "Die 'Synagoge' am Münster zu Strassburg." *Das Münster* (periodical), 1947. Page 65 et seq.
[2] Josef Sauer, *Symbolik des Kirchengebäudes und seiner Austattung* . . . Frieburg i Br., 1902. Page 52.

character of the system of allegorical and symbolic interpretation. In French scholarship, the books of Emile Mâle,
which expound the whole wealth of mediaeval pictorial art, are
specially important.[1] We owe much to his profound understanding of twelfth- and thirteenth-century iconography.

The question now arises whether mediaeval theologists
applied their allegorical-symbolical methods of interpretation to the church as a building. The answer is "yes", but at
first there was nothing exclusively applicable to the Gothic
church. The explanations and similes of mediaeval symbolism are equally valid for Christian church building in
general and go back to early Christian times. Among these
was the identification of the "church" with "Jerusalem".
The example of Jerusalem was often used to explain the
fourfold significance of holy writ. "Jerusalem = a city in
Judaea; allegorical = the church on earth; tropological
= man's soul; anagogical = the kingdom of eternal bliss.[2]
In this realm of mediaeval church symbolism the periodic
stylistic changes in ecclesiastical architecture, obvious to us
in retrospect, played no part. We must therefore distinguish
various gradations of meaning in the mediaeval conception
of Gothic cathedrals, which, in connection with the traditional symbolism of God's house, have survived in a greater
or lesser degree.

The anthropomorphous view of the church building,
linked with the interpretation of the church as the mystical
body of Christ, was very commonly held. For Durandus the
church was shaped like a kind of human body, a comparison
which could only be applied to the cruciform ground plan,
that is to say, to a church with transepts. The altar and choir
represented the head, the transepts were the two arms and
the nave signified the body with legs and feet. On the other
hand, this ground plan transformed into a human being
could equally well reflect the enduring nature of the Christian
community. Even the building stones, the walls, the windows, the separation of the houses of priest and laymen

---

[1] Emile Mâle, *L'Art religieux du XIIe siècle en France.* 3rd edition. Paris,
1928. *L'Art religieux du XIIIe siècle en France.* 6th edition. Paris, 1925.
[2] Jos. Sauer, *Symbolik des Kirchengebäudes.* 1902. Page 103.

would be drawn into this allegorical system. The variety of symbolic interpretation was so great that we can only indicate the general trend of mediaeval thinking.

The survival of the symbolism of individual structural components in church architecture into the period of the Gothic cathedrals can be definitely established in certain cases. The anthropomorphous conception of columns as human forms is old and easy to accept, especially since we sometimes talk of the column's head and its foot. It found its way into Christian architectural symbolism and appears in Abbot Suger's writings (1081–1151).

The personality of Abbot Suger has exceptional significance for us, because he has told the story from the client's point of view of a new building which he initiated, and which architectural history has been accustomed to regard as the first example of Gothic style.[1] This was the choir of St. Denis (1140–1144), of which the lower part, at any rate, has been preserved. Characteristically, Abbot Suger does not mention the architect, although the building deserves its reputation.[2] Far more important, however, is what Suger, as the client and patron, thought specially significant. As an answer to our question about the symbolic interpretation of particular building elements, let us turn by way of example to the passage describing the building, where Suger says: "In the middle twelve columns rose, corresponding to the number of the Apostles, and the same number in the side aisles, according to the words of the Apostle, who built in the spirit: '. . . ye are no more strangers and foreigners, but fellow-citizens with the Saints and of the Household of God; built upon the foundation of the Apostles and prophets, Jesus Christ himself being the chief corner-stone; in whom all the building fitly framed together groweth' spiritually and materially 'into an holy temple in the Lord'."

The connection between the piers and the Apostles and

---

[1] Cf. Erwin Panofsky, *Abbot Suger*. Princeton, 1946. Otto v. Simson. *The Gothic Cathedral*. London and New York, 1956.

[2] In addition to earlier judgments in Dehio (1892), Gall (1925), Sedlmayr (1950), compare also the architectural appraisal of Sumner McK. Crosby in *L'Abbaye Royale de St. Denis*. Paris, 1953. Page 44 et seq.; also of Otto v. Simson in the book frequently mentioned above.

prophets is confined to their number, which had great symbolic importance in the middle ages, and in the context above the columns mentioned by Suger refer only to the piers round the choir and in the ambulatory, those therefore which surround the area of the altar. Whether this twelfth-century mode of reasoning should be interpreted as "visible" or "theoretical" symbolism is hard to decide. In the high middle ages there were certainly various points of view on this matter. A learned clerk like Durandus set out his allegorical and symbolic interpretation in accordance with his knowledge of tradition, pondering each gradation of meaning theologically, seated, as it were, at his desk. But in a great churchman and architectural patron like Abbot Suger, with a deep appreciation of the arts, we can detect something of the symbolism which is experienced and seen. With him the ecclesia materialis and spiritualis were closely linked. Like St. Paul he built "spiritually", while he also erected "materially" the choir of St. Denis. Nevertheless we cannot accept that he himself was responsible for the design. He worked on the building with his architect, but we know nothing of the kind of understanding which existed between clients and architects. This question has already been touched upon in an earlier chapter with reference to the decision by the Master of Chartres to dispense with the traditional tribune galleries used in early Gothic cathedrals. It is reasonable to suppose that the bishop and chapter agreed, but it is out of the question that they contributed to the conception of the new elevational system. They could only "approve" the novel ideas of a brilliant architect, a point which should not be underrated.

Meaning and Form

G. Bandmann, to whom we are indebted in the field of recent scholarship for an instructive analysis of the meaning of mediaeval architecture, has raised this question in his exposition of the above passage from Abbot Suger: "Can the allegorical interpretation have consequences to form, whether by emphasizing particular elements or by representing a different thing and using it metaphorically?"[1]

In general we are bound to admit that mediaeval theologians superimposed a meaning upon the church and its component members afterwards. But it is by no means clear that in the middle ages men had any sense that there was a definite symbolic meaning in what they built, for in planning a vast number of considerations had to be taken into account, which are never mentioned in mediaeval symbolism. Moreover, Abbot Suger does not refer to traditions of structural form or to embarking upon the design of a particular type of choir in his new building at St. Denis. In the formulation of a great plan, an architectural and spatial conception linked with tradition, and the symbolic reasoning behind it, may combine and complement one another in the architect and the client, without our being able to separate the individual factors. The creative process, which is a secret of the birth of a work of art, eludes analysis.

Bandmann gives his answer: "We must therefore say that the allegorical interpretation can have an effect on form by moulding it to portray the meaning attributed to it, but it can also have no effect on form whatever."[2]

That the columnae mentioned by Suger in the choir of St. Denis contained an inherent symbolism, which survived long after, seems to be suggested by the fact that during the thirteenth century allegorical meaning was still conveyed in material form. The classic cathedrals admittedly displayed no monumental sculpture in the interior (with the exception of the decoration of the choir screen), but in the Sainte-Chapelle in Paris (1245–1248) there appear for the first time on the piers figures of Apostles facing the interior, while at the beginning of the fourteenth century we find in the choir of Cologne Cathedral pillars which, with the increasing size of High Gothic "orders", can hardly be considered anthropomorphous any longer, adorned with statues of the twelve Apostles and still reflecting those "spiritually"

---

[1] Günter Bandmann, *Mittelalterliche Architektur als Bedeutungsträger*. Berlin, 1951. Page 67.
[2] Bandmann. Page 70.

seen associations which Suger assigns to them in his description of the choir of St. Denis.

The Whole Building seen as the City of Heaven

The most important question which we have to consider with reference to the symbolism of Gothic cathedrals, is that of the entire building in the anagogical sense according to mediaeval interpretation. Here too we shall refer first to interpretations which are valid for Western Christian church building as a whole, and not for individual periods. All mediaeval authors are agreed that the church, as a building, represents the City of God, the heavenly Jerusalem. This theory goes back to early Christian times and is based on the description in the Revelation of St. John: "And I John saw the holy city, new Jerusalem, coming down from God out of heaven, prepared as a bride adorned for her husband. And I heard a great voice out of heaven saying, Behold, the tabernacle of God is with men, and he will dwell with them, and they shall be his people, and God himself shall be with them, and be their God." Further on in the same chapter the holy city is described in all its radiant majesty. "The heavenly Jerusalem, the glorious city of God, in which God himself has raised his tabernacle in the midst of mankind, is the ideal which is reflected in a Christian church building. It needs no reference to the countless utterances of early scriptural commentators to accept that this description of the Apocalypse (xxi, verse 2 et seq.) is a picture of God's Kingdom and of the Church in her ultimate fulfilment; the author of this vision most certainly had nothing else in mind. In the complex inter-relationship between the Church in a material sense and the Church spiritual, however, it was inevitable that this description should also be applied to the church as a building and that its spiritual implication should thus become material. It has already been pointed out above that, in the consecration address of the church of Tyre, the church building is represented as the tangible image of an invisible kingdom. What makes this declaration so momentous is the occasion which inspired it, the consecration of a new house of God. From this we become acquainted with the movement at the beginning of the fourth century, which sanctioned liturgically, by its acceptance in the rite of dedication, the comparison of the church building with the heavenly Jerusalem as the perfect picture of the spiritual Church, and used it for this purpose in innumerable sermons and hymns."[1]

The question as to how these visionary theories are reflected in the church buildings of different centuries, which architectural history offers us, has been very variously answered. Lothar Kitschelt has pointed out that the early Christian basilica, in its representation of the heavenly Jerusalem, derives, so far as its principal features are concerned, from the Hellenistic idea of the city.[2] For the mediaeval centuries, then, the question found no consistent solution, for notions about cities change and it must be accepted that Romanesque church architecture, too, depended upon changed conceptions of the city in its representation of the heavenly Jerusalem.[3] That the city idea was still echoed also in the Gothic cathedral, at least in the entrance front, to the extent that in the twin-towered façade with its three portal openings is a veiled representation of the city gate, is established. Kitschelt has referred to this[4] and recently Otto von Simson, in discussing the gate symbol, has found a source for the façade of St. Denis in the reconstruction of the Roman gate at Cologne.[5]

The interpretation of the church portal as the entrance to heaven is founded not only upon the conception of the whole building as the city of God, but in the case of St. Denis, for example, on the evidence of Abbot Suger,[6] while it is also expressed symbolically in portal sculpture by the Last Judgment. In this context there is an obvious significance in placing the cycle of the Wise and Foolish Virgins on the door jambs and in the reference to the entrance as the

---

[1] J. Sauer, *Symbolik des Kirchengebäudes*. Page 103.
[2] Lothar Kitschelt, *Die frühchristliche Basilika als Darstellung des himmlischen Jerusalem*. Munich, 1938. Cf. also Bandmann, page 89 et seq.
[3] Cf. Bandmann, page 85 et seq.   [4] Kitschelt. Page 35.
[5] v. Simson. Page 109.
[6] Panofsky, *Abbot Suger*. Page 46. Bandmann. Page 81.

porta coeli. In the monumental sculpture of Gothic cathedrals, like Paris and Amiens, the Wise and Foolish Virgins
stand on both sides of the jambs of the middle portal,
following the iconographical arrangement of St. Denis.

Image—Symbol—Work of Art

Hans Sedlmayr has gone further than anybody in pursuing
the symbolic meaning of the church as a building. He sees
the Gothic cathedral not only in the anagogical sense as the
heavenly Jerusalem, but recognizes in it a visible, tangible
image of the City of God revealed in the vision of the
Apocalypse. "For the purpose of transplanting the visitor,
so to speak, 'really' into the City of God, the early Christian
church building stands closer to the Gothic cathedral than
either do to the Romanesque cathedral, the significance of
which does not yield so readily to comparative analysis, but
remains more deeply enveloped in clouds of mystery. Whilst
in the early Christian basilica, however, it is the 'city-
factor' of the City of God which is primarily represented, here
[the Gothic cathedral] the heavenly-factor of the heavenly
building, and the light-factor of the city of light, are
dramatically depicted with every means that art can devise.
Value is not so much laid on the city-like appearance of the
church—the traditional form of Gothic building with its
cruciform ground plan is far from resembling a city—but on
poetical characteristics. . . . These characteristics must be
borne in mind if we want to understand clearly how the
cathedral was able to convey to people of the time not
merely a sense of heaven in the mind's eye, but to bring it
actually into physical view. . . ." "The Gothic cathedral
gave tangible form to a poetic interpretation of the architecture of heaven—first and foremost in the interior, but
with the outside, too, woven into the complete picture. In it
the visual and plastic arts contend with the heavenly
metaphors of religious poetry, which they far surpass."[1]

However overwhelming the impression of a supraworldly
quality in this sacred architecture, which the majestic float-

[1] Hans Sedlmayr, *Die Entstehung der Kathedrale.* 1950. Page 234 et seq.

ing space of the interior produces by its weightlessness, towering verticality and diaphanous structure, however exquisitely contrived in these respects the "poetical" conception, none the less the Gothic cathedral, a work of art which emerged in a clearly defined area and period of history, cannot have derived from the mind of a poet the wonderful structural logic with which it was erected in widely varying forms, nor the precision of detail which may be described as the mathematics of the classic cathedral.

But even if we lay aside the "imagery" in the literal sense of the word, there remains the high symbolic power of the Gothic cathedral. Without this quality it could not have decided the style of ecclesiastical architecture for the entire Western world until the end of the middle ages. The Gothic cathedral was the product of tireless endeavours by a succession of twelfth- and thirteenth-century masters of genius, who by their architecture gave material form to our conception of a supramundane world which could be seen and felt. It was the architecture which exercised this symbolic power, and we are struck with wonder by the realization that the words with which the Bible praises the creator of the world can apply to the master-designer of a cathedral in his work of creation as well: "omnia in mensura et numero et pondere disposuisti."[1]

[1] The Wisdom of Solomon, ch. 11, v. 20, " . . . thou hast ordered all things in measure and number and weight."

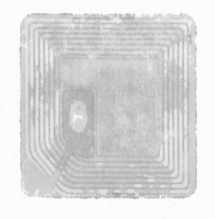